The Best of **WOODCARVING**
ILLUSTRATED

MW00527716

RELIEF CARVING

PROJECTS & TECHNIQUES

The Best of WOODCARVING
ILLUSTRATED

RELIEF CARVING

PROJECTS & TECHNIQUES

Expert Advice and 37 All-Time Favorite Projects and Patterns

From the Editors of *Woodcarving Illustrated*

Winter Lighthouse,
by Robert Stadtlander,
page 63

FOX CHAPEL
PUBLISHING

© 2011 by Fox Chapel Publishing Company, Inc., 903 Square Street, Mount Joy, PA 17552.

Patterns on pages 51 and 52 © 2011 by Kathy Wise Designs Inc.

ISBN 978-1-56523-558-8

Library of Congress Cataloging-in-Publication Data

Relief carving projects & techniques / from the editors of Woodcarving illustrated.

    p. cm. -- (The best of Woodcarving illustrated)

Includes index.

ISBN 978-1-56523-558-8

1. Wood-carving. I. Wood carving illustrated. II. Title: Relief carving projects and techniques.

TT199.7.R46 2011

736'.4--dc22

               2010049440

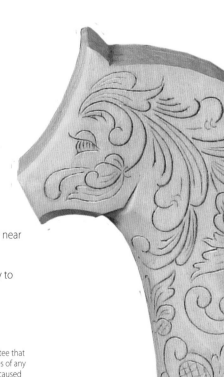

To learn more about the other great books from Fox Chapel Publishing, or to find a retailer near
you, call toll-free 800-457-9112 or visit us at *www.FoxChapelPublishing.com*.

We are always looking for talented authors. To submit an idea, please send a brief inquiry to
acquisitions@foxchapelpublishing.com.

Printed in China
Fourth printing

Table of Contents

What You Can Make

Spring/ Summer

Flowers, page 32

Door, page 43

Fruit, page 57

Chickens, page 61

Sunflower, page 82

Bridge, page 127

Eagle, page 137

Lighthouse, page 139

Greenman, page 140

Fall

Duck, page 10

Deer, page 16

Barn, page 40

Leaves, page 88

Barn, page 129

Acorn, page 131

Harvester, page 132

Duck, page 138

Winter

Snowman, page 36

Lighthouse, page 63

Poinsettias, page 75

Angel, page 118

Santa and snowman, page 133

Any Season

Santa, page 134

Horn, page 135

Lamb and puppy, page 136

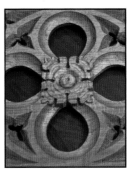
Trivet, page 24

Egg, page 30

Bulldog, page 47

Color guard, page 70

Blocks, page 96

Sign, page 100

House sign, page 104

Plaque, page 112

Knotwork, page 124

Hearts, page 125

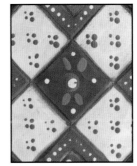
Quilt, page 126

Home Sweet Home, page 141

Getting Started

There's no substitute for experience—especially if you can borrow someone else's. In this chapter, experienced carvers including Lora S. Irish, Chuck Solomon, and Dave Hamilton share the tips and techniques they have developed over the years. The lessons they have to teach include how to accurately measure carving levels; how to glue up carving panels so they don't bend; how to use power tools and woodburning in your relief carving; and how to translate a two-dimensional pattern into a three-dimensional work of art.

Pintail Duck,
by Chuck Solomon and
Dave Hamilton,
page 10

Power Carving in Relief

By Chuck Solomon and Dave Hamilton

This basic relief project combines techniques for using reciprocating tools, traditional-edge tools, rotary bits, and a woodburner. If you don't have a reciprocating handpiece, use a piece of scrap wood to practice lowering the background with aggressive carbide-point bits in a rotary power carver.

The northern pintail duck can be found throughout North America and northern areas of Europe and Asia. We have both had the opportunity to view and study pintail ducks at numerous national wildlife refuges and other wetland areas. It is a thrill to see hundreds of pintails rise off the water early in the morning.

We chose a slab of basswood with bark remaining on the sides to provide a natural frame. Use graphite paper to transfer the pattern to the blank and sketch an oval around the design. Leave at least ¼" (6mm) between the oval and any part of the duck.

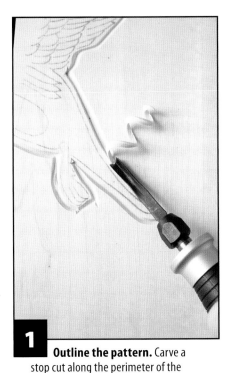

1 **Outline the pattern.** Carve a stop cut along the perimeter of the pattern with a ¼" (6mm)-wide V-tool in a reciprocating carver. Cut approximately ⅛" (3mm) outside of the pattern line.

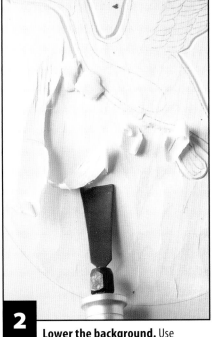

2 **Lower the background.** Use a ¾" (19mm)-wide fishtail gouge in a reciprocating carver to lower the area between the oval and the pattern. Remove the wood in several passes. Reposition the blank as needed to make the smoothest cuts. Slope the wood from the oval to the cuts next to the duck.

3 **Clean up the gouge marks.** Go back over the background with the same fishtail gouge to clean up and smooth the surface. Switch to a handheld ¾" (19mm)-wide fishtail gouge to provide more control, especially near the duck.

4 **Separate the wings.** Carve along the line separating the wings with a V-tool in the reciprocating carver. Use a fishtail gouge to lower the back wing slightly, creating the effect of the back wing being behind the front wing.

5 **Round the duck's body.** Round the body with a pear-shaped stump cutter in the flexible shaft tool. Use a high speed (14,000 rpm or greater) for best control. Clean up the edges by hand sanding with 250-grit Swiss sanding cloth. Do not round the wing tips.

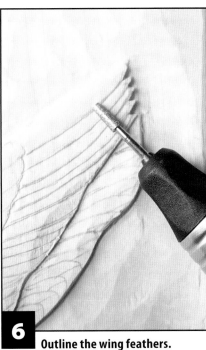

6 **Outline the wing feathers.** Remove the wood between the tips of the feathers with a bench knife or a safe-end cylinder-shaped diamond bit and a flame-shaped ruby or diamond bit. Make a shallow stop cut alongside each wing feather with a bench knife. Carve between each feather with a safe-end cylinder-shaped diamond bit.

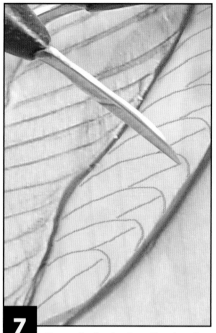

7 **Carve the back wing.** Sketch in the feathers on the back wing. The front wing shows the underside of the wing and full top primary feathers. On the back wing, we are viewing the top of the wing and only see part of the top primary feathers. Stop-cut along each feather with a bench knife and carve between the feathers with a safe-end cylinder-shaped diamond bit.

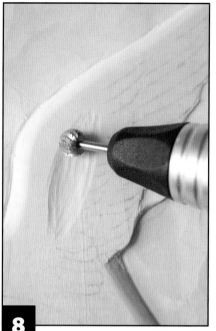

8 **Carve a depression in the front wing.** Use a ½" (13mm)-diameter ball-shaped stump cutter to carve a shallow depression in the front wing. The ¼" (6mm)-deep depression, located in front of the covert feathers, should be less than 1" (25mm) wide.

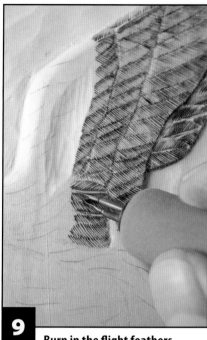

9 **Burn in the flight feathers.** Woodburn the primary, secondary, tertial, and covert feathers on the wings. Use a ⅜" (10mm)-wide skew-tip woodburning pen. Keep the burn lines curved at the top and keep them as close together as possible.

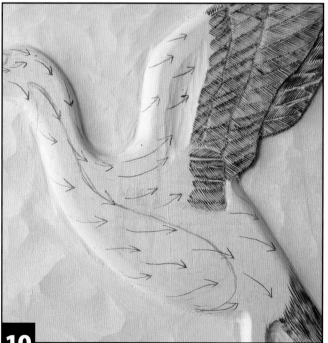

10 **Sketch the body feathers.** Outline the location of the back tail feathers, rump, white body feathers of the lower breast and body, the brown feathers on the head and neck, and the dark feathers on the back and sides. Sketch in the direction of the feather flow.

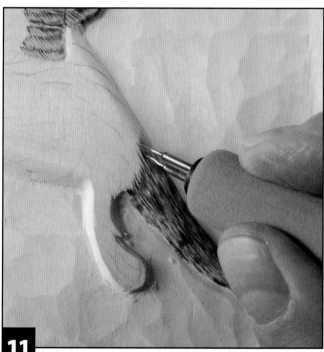

11 **Woodburn the body feathers.** Use a higher temperature to burn the black tail feathers and rump. Keep these lines close to each other. The darker body feathers are burned at a lower temperature and are farther apart. The white feather areas are burned at an even lower temperature and the lines are even farther apart.

Photocopy at 100%
or desired size

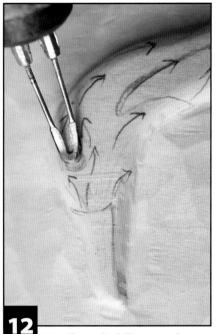

12 **Woodburn the bill, eye, and foot.** Use a ⅛" (3mm)-wide shader burning pen for the bill and the foot. Outline and burn the eye with a writing tip burning pen.

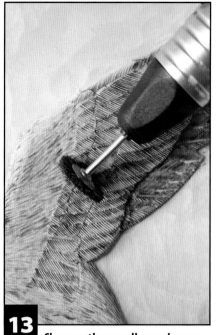

13 **Clean up the woodburned areas.** Use a soft rotary brush in the flexible shaft tool at a low speed (less than 5,000 rpm) to remove any residue left from the woodburning pens. Brush in the direction of the burning. Strengthen the feather tips and any other areas that could break with thin cyanoacrylate (CA) glue.

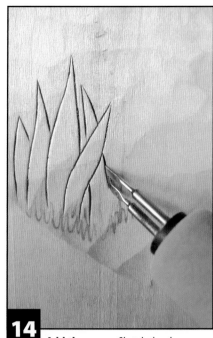

14 **Add the grass.** Sketch the clump of wetland grass or other vegetation on a copy of the pattern and then transfer the design to the blank. Use a skew woodburning pen to burn in the grass.

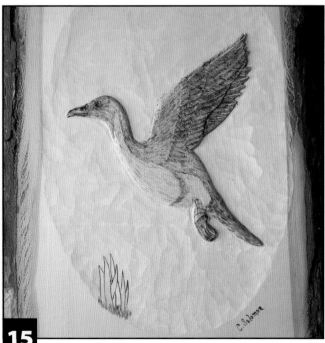

15 **Apply the finish.** Apply a light coat of satin finish spray. Let it dry for 15 to 45 minutes. Go over the duck with a soft rotary brush at a low speed (less than 5,000 rpm). Apply one to two additional coats, allowing it to dry between coats. Use a soft rotary brush on the duck between coats and after you apply the final coat. Attach a hanger to the back of the carving.

Materials & Tools

Materials:
- 1" x 10" x 14" (25mm x 254mm x 356mm) basswood or wood of choice
- Swiss sanding cloth, 250 grit
- Thin cyanoacrylate glue
- Satin-finish spray lacquer

Tools:
- Flexible-shaft machine with a standard handpiece
- Reciprocating carver or handpiece
- Reciprocating gouges: ¾" (20mm) fishtail gouge and ¼" (6mm)-wide V-tool
- ¼" (6mm)-diameter ball-shaped stump cutter
- ¼" (6mm)-diameter pear-shaped stump cutter
- Safe-end cylinder-shaped diamond bit
- Flame-shaped ruby or diamond bit
- Soft rotary bristle brush
- Woodburner
- ⅜" (10mm)-wide skew tip burning pen
- ⅜" (10mm)-wide shader burning pen
- Writing tip burning pen
- ¾" (20mm) fishtail palm gouge
- Carving knife of choice

Relief Carver's Depth Finder

By Jim Dupont

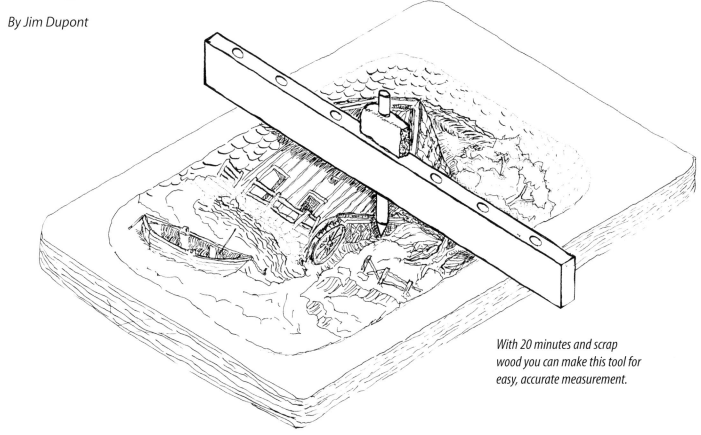

With 20 minutes and scrap wood you can make this tool for easy, accurate measurement.

Carvers who work in deep relief need to know the depth they are carving at when working on a project. The typical method is to put a straight edge on the surface of the work and use a ruler set at a right angle to it to measure the depth. Unfortunately, this results in two possible errors. First, because of the ruler's width, you cannot always be certain that it is touching the deepest part of the area being measured. Second, it is difficult to read the ruler owing to the angle you are viewing it from. As a result, you are likely to get inaccurate measurements.

My design eliminates both problems. A dowel rod with a pointed tip reaches all the way to the bottom surface. It can then be removed, and the measurements taken from the dowel. It is simple and inexpensive: You can make it in less than 20 minutes using a length of scrap wood, an eraser (rubber works, but a large gum one is ideal), a section of hardwood dowel (¼", ⁵⁄₁₆", and ⅜" [6mm, 8mm, and 10mm] diameters all work well), a saw, a power drill and drill bit, and a pencil sharpener.

To construct the depth finder, select a narrow board with a straight edge. Mine measures ½" thick by 1½" wide by 18" long (13mm by 40mm by 460mm). Cut off a section of dowel that will accommodate the width of the board plus the deepest penetration you expect to make into the relief carving. Add a couple of extra inches for the eraser and a handhold. To make the point, sharpen one end in a pencil sharpener. The dowel I use is 5" (125mm) long.

Drill holes slightly larger than the diameter of the dowel in the edge of the board every 2" (50mm). These allow you to take depth readings at all areas of the carving. Drill a hole the same diameter as the dowel in the eraser; this provides a stop gauge while holding the dowel in place.

You can make a pencil mark on the dowel as a reference or mark lines on the dowel as you would find on a ruler.

Working with Relief Carving Patterns

By Lora S. Irish

I provide as much information as possible in my line drawing patterns, and many other designers do the same. However, to successfully transform a two-dimensional drawing into a three-dimensional relief carving, you should view patterns as starting points.

Taking the time to work with a pattern before you pick up your gouges and chisels can make the carving work easier and the finished product more dramatic. It may sound complicated, but it's not. Here's how I do it.

Prepare the Pattern

Before you begin any carving project, gather reference material on the subject. Photos and drawings of the live animal, bird, person, or landscape provide important information that helps you make the best possible pattern and pattern notations.

To make a tracing carving pattern from a detailed pattern drawing, reduce the pattern to its simplest form. Do this by placing a sheet of tracing paper over your pattern and copying only those lines that define a given area and places where there are major contour changes. Compare Figure 1 and Figure 2, paying particular attention to how I simplified the fence post area.

Figure 1. Full Pattern Detail

Figure 2. Simplified Pattern

Next, create a contour drawing of the major design elements to help you understand how to shape individual areas and how they interact with adjacent areas. Using a copy of your simplified pattern and a soft pencil, darken the sides and edges of each area where you will sculpt the area during the carving. The deeper you think you will carve, the darker you sketch into that area. See Figure 3.

Many patterns contain a directional flow, either in the space that contains the pattern or a repetitive angle found throughout the subject. The flow is very important when placing the wood blank.

Figure 4 shows the *V*-flow that repeats in this pattern. All of the *V*-points fall at the central vertical line, so you need to make sure the central line is at a true 90° angle to the blank. Tilting this pattern away from the central line of the blank would make the finished carving look lopsided.

Figure 3. Contour Details

Figure 4. Directional Flow

With the flow lines noted, it's time to establish levels—determine which elements of the composition need to be closest to the viewer and which ones will be farthest away. Begin by grouping elements into units according to their depth. Figure 5 shows the five distinct elements in this pattern: fence post, grasses, rocks, fur areas, and antlers. Each will be carved with its own style of texturing.

Figure 5. Levels

The fence post lies behind every other element within the pattern, so it is the first, deepest level. The shoulder area of the buck, which projects above the post, is the second level. On top of the shoulders lies the main section of the neck; this will be the third level. In front of the neck are the ears, the connecting section of the neck, and the eye and forehead section of the face, which are level four. The muzzle of the buck is level five.

Some elements flow from one level into another. Here, the antlers at the base of the skull are behind the face, but the antler tips arch forward over the muzzle. The ears are established in the level of the eye sockets, but may jut forward or be tilted back toward the neck. Make a pencil notation on your pattern where an individual element might change levels. Once all your notations are made, trace the simplified pattern onto the wood blank.

Carve the Pattern

The basic process is the same for any relief pattern. Keep your pencil sharp and handy because as you remove wood, you will continually need to refresh pattern lines and other notations, such as the *V* flow that repeats in this one, as shown in Figure 4. The following steps show the process required to make the mule deer head.

1   **Establish the background depth.** Mark the interior or trapped areas of the background with a pencil so you can easily find them as you rough out the work. Use a large V-gouge to establish the outer edges of the design, creating sloped walls that also provide extra room to maneuver your tools during the contouring stage.

2   **Mark the levels.** Using a pencil, mark each element with its respective level number. Notice the darkened line that separates the shoulder and neck levels, and the one that separates the muzzle from the eye sockets.

3   **Rough out the levels.** The fence post, rocks, and grasses have become one unit. Each level is fairly flat at this stage, with all elements within that level roughed out to the same depth. In this photo, the tip of his right ear is back away from his face. The antlers at the top of his skull are deeply set into level two but the tips reach upward into level five with his muzzle.

4 **Reestablish pattern lines.** Cut your simplified pattern into sections and tape each section individually to the wood. Slide a small piece of tracing paper under that section and retrace your working lines.

5 **Contour each element within a level.** In this photo, the general contouring work in the fence post area is completed. Note that because this section was originally carved as a unit, all the elements within that unit lie behind the buck's shoulders. Establishing a depth for all the elements within this section of the pattern first ensures that any carving you do will be at the right depth for the overall work. At this stage the directional *V* reappears.

6 **Incorporate any mistakes into the design.** My original drawing showed a barbed wire fence, but I lost the barbed *X*'s that were part of the wire and so turned it into rope. We all make mistakes, but as in this case, you can often integrate them into the design with a few adjustments.

Work from the background to the foreground as you sculpt each element. The shoulders, neck, ears, and antlers are starting to take shape. You can see the reduction of the antler on his right side at this stage of work; the extra space created with the *V*-gouge has been removed.

7 **Add details.** Contouring each area makes the overall depth of the work apparent. Refer often to your contour sketch for each section as you work. Although this carving is on a ¾" (20mm) basswood board, worked at its deepest point to ⅝" (16mm), the use of levels in the early stage of carving pushes the fence post back into the scene and pulls the muzzle forward, making the carving appear deeper than it is. Add final detailing.

8 **Finish the work with a sealer or oil, varnish, or polyurethane.** At this stage, the carving can be left in the wood grain or prepared for coloring with acrylic or oil paints. Because I am adding oil colors, I applied a base coat of linseed oil mixed half-and-half with turpentine to seal the wood. If you choose to leave the carving as is at this point, apply an appropriate finish or sealer.

9 **Add the color (optional).** I chose to add color, using oil paints dry brushed across the different textures in the wood, fur, and antlers. Color lies on the surface of your contoured carving. Once the oil paint dries, add a final finish of Danish oil.

Reference photos are key to making realistic portrayals. This one is from wildlife artist Doug Lindstrand's *Deer: The Ultimate Artist's Reference.*

Photocopy at 100%

Simplified Pattern

© 2011 Woodcarving Illustrated

Photocopy at 212%

Full Detail

Gluing Up Relief Carving Panels: It's in the Camber

By W.F. (Bill) Judt

Many relief carvers have experienced the frustration of seeing a relief panel of glued-up boards warp and cup to the carved side, changing what was supposed to be a beautiful piece of craftsmanship into a cause for disappointment.

In my early years as a carver, I faced the problem many times. I sought an answer, but finding nothing, developed my own camber method. It is time-tested, reasonable, and straightforward. With it, you can construct relief panels that are dimensionally stable, attractive, and reflective of the work you put into them.

Adding Camber

Removing wood from a relief panel destabilizes the carved side of the panel. With less wood on the carved side to hold it in place, the back of the relief panel relaxes and bends toward the side with less wood, as shown in A (right). Adding camber—a slight bend similar to that in downhill skis or the leaf springs in automobiles, as shown in B (far right)—stabilizes the panel and counteracts its tendency to cup. Carving the convex side flattens the panel.

Over the years I experimented with the amount of camber needed and the degree to which various woods cup. Birch, my favorite relief carving wood, tends to cup moderately; basswood and mahogany tend to cup less. I have not found wood suitable for relief carving that does not cup to the carved side.

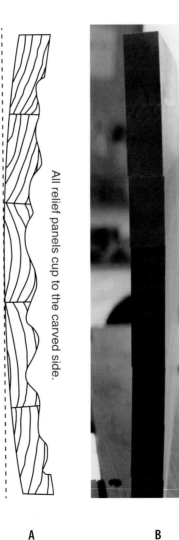

All relief panels cup to the carved side.

A   B

Building Camber

To build camber into relief panels, prepare a number of pieces of wood for lamination. Cut them to length, rip them to widths of 3" to 4", and plane them to the same thickness.

Use a pencil to mark the surface of each board that will end up on the carved side of the panel. This is typically the sapwood side of the board, because sapwood is lighter and, being closer to the bark than heartwood, has growth rings with a larger arc. I place the darker heartwood side, where the growth rings have a smaller arc that can compete with the relief in a carving, to the back of the panel.

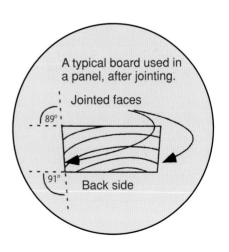

A typical board used in a panel, after jointing.

Jointed faces

89°

91°

Back side

The camber method of joining panels for relief carving requires setting a jointer fence 1° or 2° from its vertical position.

Using a Jointer

Arrange the boards as they will appear in the finished relief panel, then use a jointer to machine them for a slight barrel-stave effect.

Jointers, with flat beds and rotating blades, create straight edges on boards and straighten and smooth lumber. For most operations, a jointer fence is set at 90°, but for this, I set it at 91° or 92°—1° or 2° from its vertical position. The result is boards with angled edges; joined edge to edge, they form a slight curvature the same way wooden barrel staves do.

Joining four 4"-wide boards to create a 16"-wide relief panel results in three joints. If each cambered face is machined 1° out of

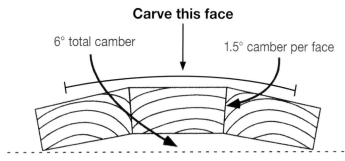

Carve this face

6° total camber

1.5° camber per face

The RIGHT way to apply camber to a panel.
Here the change in angle (exaggerated for clarity) is gradual.

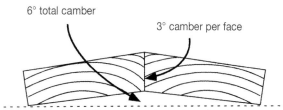

6° total camber

3° camber per face

The WRONG way to apply camber to a panel.
Here, the change in angle (exaggerated for clarity) is too severe.

square, each joint has 2° of camber built into it—so three joints means a total of 6° camber for the panel.

I use yellow carpenter's glue to glue the boards together, without the additional support of dowels or biscuits. I put pipe clamps across the boards and C clamps at each joint to keep the boards from moving out of position. After tightening the pipe clamps, you can remove the C clamps. The result is a panel that is convex on the side to be carved.

As you carve, the panel will cup to the carved side as predicted, consuming most of the built-in camber. Some camber should remain; it won't be visible if the finished carving hangs on a wall and will, in fact, help the carving hang better.

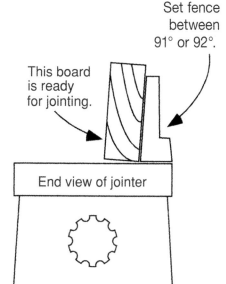

Set fence between 91° or 92°.

This board is ready for jointing.

End view of jointer

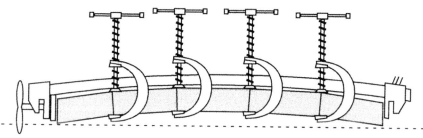

Pipe clamps and C clamps help assemble the panel.
Note the camber on the bottom side of the panel.

Relief Carving Projects

This chapter highlights the wonderful versatility of relief carving techniques. Just getting started? Simple projects like the trivet design allow you to learn the basics with hand tools while creating attractive pieces. Looking to challenge your time-honed skills? Flip toward the end, where advanced projects like the deep-relief mantel use power tools to create truly stunning results. Want a piece to celebrate your favorite season? Start with a Grand Old Flag egg or a brilliant, snowy lighthouse. Need a way to thank someone who protects you? The color guard figure can be customized for different branches of the military or emergency services. And there's more; prepare to be inspired.

Country Charm Quilt Squares, by Lora S. Irish, page 57

Trivet Designs

By Frederick Wilbur

These designs are inspired by classic Gothic tracery used to support glass in large windows.

These beautifully functional trivets give you the opportunity to practice making clean cuts and sharp corners. They require only a few gouges and minimal investment of time and materials, which makes them ideal for holiday gift giving.

These trivets are inspired by classic Gothic tracery. Gothic tracery is the decorative use of supports for the glass in large windows. These supports are called mullions. The configurations of the mullions were adapted to many forms of woodwork, from massive and ornate choir stalls of cathedrals to dining room chairs. These trivets reflect two popular configurations; the quatrefoil is an early design, while the whorled trefoil appeared somewhat later in the period.

The predominant species of wood used in English Gothic work is English or European white oak. I use American white oak, quartersawn for strength and stability. Using an exotic wood, such as mahogany, betrays the authenticity of the original. Chestnut or walnut are acceptable alternatives.

Part of the fun in creating these trivets is drawing the patterns and immersing myself in the circles and segments of circles that make up the designs. Patterns are provided, but I encourage you to experiment with a compass and straightedge to create your own designs based on Gothic tracery.

Start by cutting the blanks to size. Copy the patterns to the blanks using carbon paper or graphite transfer paper.

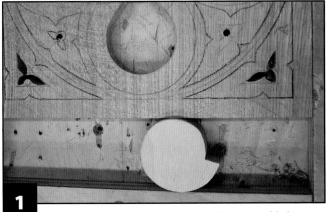

1 **Cut the pierced holes.** Drill ³⁄₁₆" (5mm)-diameter blade-entry holes and cut the open areas with a scroll saw or saber saw. Just drill a hole for the smaller open areas; we'll shape them later. Smooth the curves with sandpaper or a sanding drum. Secure the carving to a work station or between bench dogs.

2 **Rough carve the corners.** Make a stop cut from the holes toward the three corners on the valleys (the pointed arches). Use a 13mm (½") straight carver's chisel. Stab a 16mm (⅝") #8 gouge in at a slight angle at the curves of the points. Work your way around the three-cornered elements to rough in these voids.

3 **Smooth the valleys up to the corners.** I use a 13mm (½") single-bevel chisel modified to have a round nose. Work on the opposing sides simultaneously to create a clean valley. Be careful, as this tool can be difficult for a beginner to control, and the sharpened blade extends to the side of the shank. The slope of the corner trefoils may be beveled or slightly concave.

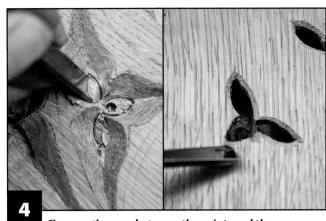

4 **Clean up the area between the points and the corners.** Use a 6mm (¼") #3 fishtail gouge. Use a 6mm (¼") #7 gouge to carve the trefoil-shaped holes. Using the same fishtail gouge, add a ⅛" (3mm)-wide bevel around the trefoil-shaped holes on the back side of the trivet. This removes any splinters created when you carved through and gives you a clean sharp edge.

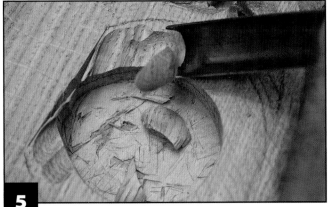

5 **Carve the coves of the circular elements (the quatrefoil).** Use a 16mm (⅝") #8 gouge and sheer with the tool as much as possible to keep the surface from looking overworked. Pay attention to the changes in grain direction.

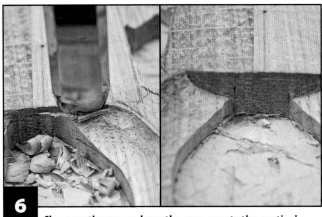

6 **Clean up the area where the cove meets the vertical wall of the flower.** Use the round-nose chisel and a 6mm (¼") #3 fishtail gouge. Pay particular attention to the areas where the grain changes.

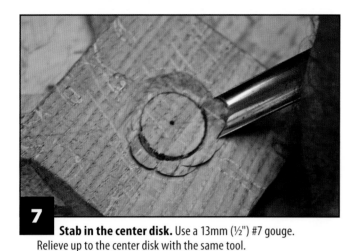

7 **Stab in the center disk.** Use a 13mm (½") #7 gouge. Relieve up to the center disk with the same tool.

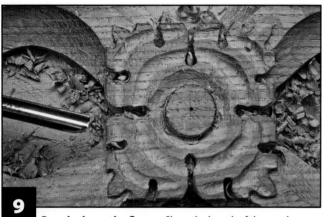

8 **Carve the four holes (eyes) between the petals.** Use a 4mm (³⁄₁₆") #9 gouge. Separate the four petals with a 13mm (½") #7 gouge.

9 **Rough-shape the flower.** Slope the length of the petals a bit to prepare for the exaggerated undulations characteristic of Gothic leaves. Use a 4mm (³⁄₁₆") #9 gouge to make a series of circular grooves that get deeper as you approach the center of the flower.

10 **Remove the edge indentions on the petals.** Use a 4mm (³⁄₁₆") #9 gouge to reduce the thickness of the wood at the edges of the petals. You want them to look slightly curved at the tips. Clean out the deep recesses with a 3mm (⅛") #3 gouge.

11 **Soften the trenches.** Use a 6mm (¼") #3 fishtail gouge turned upside down. Shape and smooth the outer edges of the petals with the same tool.

12 **Round over the center of the flower.** Use a 6mm (¼") #3 fishtail gouge. Dimple the center with a small deep gouge to add depth and dimension.

13 **Make a cove around the holes separating the petals.** To give the eyes a finished look, carve a small cove around them with a 4mm (³⁄₁₆") #9 gouge.

14 **Carve the back.** Flip the trivet over and round the edges of the coves separating the four main petals.

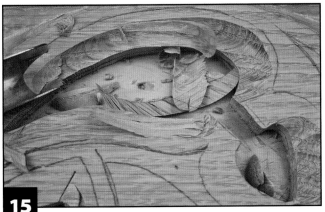

15 **Rough out the whorled design.** Use the same techniques to carve most of the valleys and shapes. Pay extra attention to the changes in grain direction.

16 **Carve the small triangle embellishments.** Use a chip carving knife or a 6mm (¼") #3 fishtail chisel. This lightens the look of the surface.

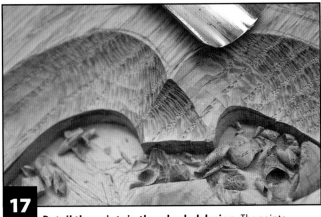

17 **Detail the points in the whorled design.** The points form an acute angle on the surface, but must be broader at the base of the cove for stability. Make a swooping triangular cut from the point of the whorl to the bottom of the cove with a round-nose chisel.

18 **Add the final details.** Drill ³⁄₈" (10mm)-diameter holes for plugs to raise the trivet above the table, or glue lengths of oak dowel into the holes. Attach cork dots to the bottom of the plugs or dowels to keep the trivet from sliding. Apply an oil finish to keep the wood clean; wax finishes will not stand up to the heat.

Quatrefoil trivet pattern

Photocopy at 100%

© 2011 Woodcarving Illustrated

MATERIALS:
- ¾" x 9" x 9" (19mm x 230mm x 230mm) white oak, chestnut, walnut, or wood of choice (per trivet)
- 4 each ⅜" (10mm)-diameter oak plugs (feet) or 4 each ⅜"(10mm)-diameter x ⅝" (15mm)-long oak dowels
- 4 each self-adhesive cork dots
- Penetrating oil finish such as Danish oil
- Carbon paper or graphite transfer paper
- Sandpaper, 80 grit (optional to smooth curves in the holes)

TOOLS:
(Gouge and chisel sizes are what I use; similar sizes and sweeps of tools will work as well.)
- 13mm (½") carver's chisel (stop cuts)
- 13mm (½") custom round-nose single-bevel chisel (cleaning acute valleys of coves)
- 6mm (¼") #3 fishtail gouge
- 3mm (⅛") or smaller #3 gouge
- #7 gouges: 6mm (¼") and 13mm (½")
- 16mm (⅝") #8 gouge

- #9 gouges: 2mm (⅛") or smaller and 4mm (³⁄₁₆")
- Chip carving knife (optional)
- Drill with ³⁄₁₆" (5mm)-diameter and ⅜" (10mm)-diameter drill bits
- Brushes and rags for finishing
- Scroll saw or saber saw
- Rotary power carver with ¼" (6mm)-diameter sanding drum (optional to smooth curves in the holes)

Whorled trefoil trivet pattern

Photocopy at 100%

© 2011 Woodcarving Illustrated

The Grand Old Flag Egg

By Linda Tudor

I designed this pattern in response to some difficult years in my country, the United States of America.

My goal was not to design a flag, but to capture an essence or a feeling. Straight stripes are fine, as in pattern B, but if you are able to create some curved ripples in the stripes, as in pattern A, they suggest the motion of a flag flying.

Remember, you are not carving an actual flag; you are carving an illusion or representation of a flag flying or draped and attempting to recall the feeling and emotion associated with it. Your view of a flag is different every time you see it, so it's not a problem if your flag eggs are not identical.

You can easily adapt the concept for the flag of your own nation or even a different subject, as the examples below show. Exercise your creativity; the elements for recognition are there, even if your interpretation is not precise.

Step 1: Select or carve an egg shape. A goose-size egg, about 2 ⅛" x 3" (55mm x 75mm), gives enough space to carve a portion of all aspects of a flag, such as the blue field, white stars, and red and white stripes.

Step 2: Sand the surface smooth. Consider how the egg will be displayed. A flat surface at the base of the egg allows it to stand upright on its own. If you don't sand a flat part, consider putting it on a stand.

Step 3: Sketch the pattern onto the surface with a pencil. Start with the stars. Don't be too concerned with size, proportion, or the number of stars or stripes. Your goal is to make it immediately identifiable, not to reproduce every detail. Orient the five-pointed stars in rows. Note that stripes run parallel to the blue field on the bottom and perpendicular on the right border.

Step 4: Carve the star edges. Use a chip-style cut. Start with the knife edge nearly 90° to the wood surface at the star edge. Make your stop cut, then cut at an angle back toward the star edges to remove the chips.

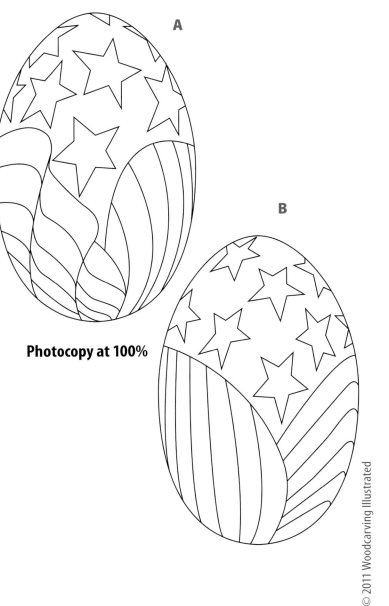

Photocopy at 100%

▲ **Step 5:** Remove any remaining material between the stars. Use a gouge to achieve the proper depth, then texture the area of the blue background with a small V-tool. This differentiates it from the smooth star surface and holds the dark color well.

Step 6: Carve lines between the stripes. Use a small V-tool or a chip carving knife where you want a sharper division. These lines will divide the colors and prevent the paint from bleeding.

Step 7: Finish the eggs. I use lacquer, oil, or wax for a natural wood look; acrylic paint for clear, brilliant colors (especially white); and oil paint thinned with linseed oil for a faded look.

MATERIALS:
- Basswood goose egg, 2⅛" x 3" (55mm x 75mm)
- Sanding cloth, 80, 220, & 400 grits
- Acrylic paints or finish of your choice

Materials & Tools

TOOLS:
- Chip carving knife
- ⁵⁄₁₆" (8mm) #7 palm gouge
- ⁵⁄₃₂" (4mm) 90° palm V-tool
- Pencil
- Eraser
- Flexible ruler

Kolrosing: Norwegian Line Carving

By Judy Ritger

Kolrosing is a Norwegian tradition of decorating wood by incising a fine line onto the surface. It means painting (rosing) with coal dust (kol). Kolrosing is mainly used on smaller objects, such as spoons, boxes, and tankards.

I learned about Norwegian folk art at the Vesterheim Norwegian-American Museum in Decorah, Iowa. I was also fortunate enough to participate in three study tours to Norway. On one of them Ragnavald Froysadal, a master painter and carver, taught me the art of kolrosing. The technique is easy to learn—the challenge comes when you start producing your own designs and patterns.

Start by choosing your wood. The clear, even grain of basswood makes it a good choice for beginners. Maple and birch are harder and take detail better, but are more tiring to carve. Start by sanding the blank with 150-grit sandpaper and work your way up to 600-grit. Spray the blank with water or rubbing alcohol, allow it to dry, and sand again with 600-grit sandpaper. This gives you a smooth surface for pattern transfer and also keeps the darkening agent from sticking to the background. Practice the technique on scrap wood before beginning on your project.

1 **Transfer the pattern to the blank.** Make a tracing of the pattern and cut out the inner circle and the outer ring. Place a piece of graphite paper under the inner circle pattern, and trace the design onto the plate. Place a piece of graphite paper under the outer ring, and trace the border onto the rim.

2 **Find a comfortable working position.** I put the plate in my lap with my feet propped up on a footstool. This allows me to lean over the piece for a better view. When the knife is in a vertical position and both hands are used to move the blade along, it can be hard to keep an open line of vision.

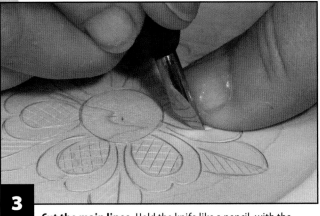

3 **Cut the main lines.** Hold the knife like a pencil, with the sharp edge away from you. Keeping the knife at an almost vertical angle, insert the blade into the wood 1⁄32" (1mm). Place your left thumb (if you are right-handed) against the back of the blade, and push the knife slowly along, using the left upper corner of your thumb as a pivot point for maximum leverage.

4 **Cut the tightly curved lines.** Use the same pushing technique, but lift up on the tip of the knife slightly as you go around a curve. Lifting the blade allows a smoother cut. Continue to use the thumb of your opposing hand to guide the cut and provide the proper leverage. Practice the cuts on scrap wood before moving on to your project.

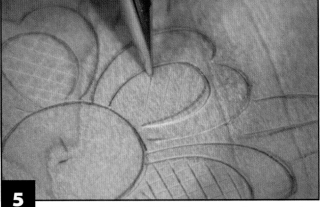

5 **Add the straight detail lines.** The push cut demonstrated above is the preferred cut in kolrosing. Some artists use the pull cut for short, straight lines, such as the hatching pattern in this design. Grip the knife like a pencil with the sharp edge toward you and gently pull the blade along the pattern line. Keep the cuts more shallow than previous cuts.

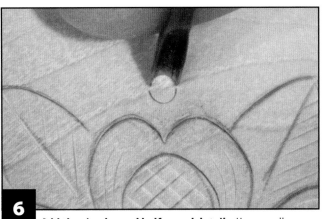

6 **Add the circular and half-round details.** Use a small semi-circular gouge to add the circles to the inside part of the plate and outer rim. Use a larger gouge to add the border between the inner plate and outer rim. Push the gouge straight into the wood, and bring it back out. The bevel of the tool creates a line that will hold the darkening agent.

7 **Add the darkening agent.** In the past, kolrosing artists sanded pine bark to produce a fine dust that they rubbed into the cuts. Finely ground or instant coffee works just as well, and it's a lot easier to find. Pick up the coffee with your fingers, and rub it into the lines. Remove the excess with paper towels. Make sure all of the lines are filled with coffee.

8 **Force the coffee deep into the lines.** Sand the surface with 400-grit sandpaper to settle the coffee into the lines and smooth down any edges raised up by the incising. Then sand with 600-grit sandpaper until the piece looks clean. Some of the coffee forced into the grain of the wood may remain, but this adds color to the whole piece. The pattern will appear faint after sanding.

9 **Apply an oil finish.** I use walnut oil or Danish oil. Apply a liberal coat of oil with a brush or your fingers. Allow the oil to soak in until the wood is saturated; then wipe off the excess. Allow the oil to dry overnight, then apply a second coat. Wipe off the excess, and allow it to dry thoroughly. Apply your chosen wax or thin polyurethane finish and buff with a soft cloth.

Embellishing with Kolrosing

It is easy to transfer a kolrosing design to a flat object, such as a plate, with graphite paper. But other objects require you to draw the design right onto the wood with a pencil.

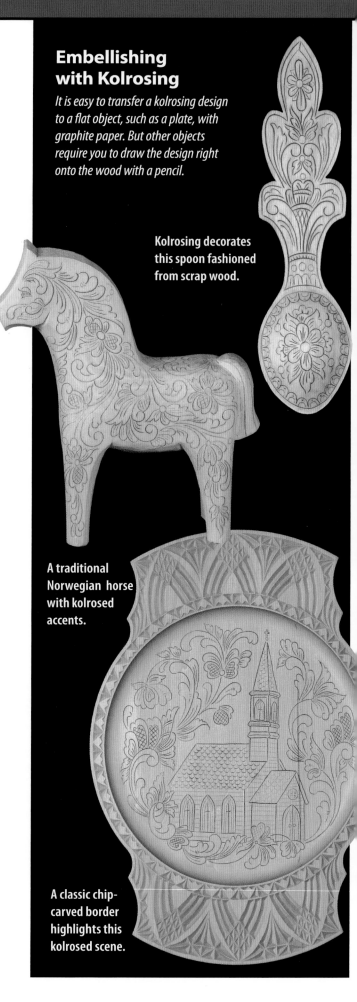

Kolrosing decorates this spoon fashioned from scrap wood.

A traditional Norwegian horse with kolrosed accents.

A classic chip-carved border highlights this kolrosed scene.

The Kolrosing Knife

Kolrosing requires a uniquely shaped knife. The short knife blade, made from high-speed steel, is shaped into a long bevel with a slight arc. The long, round handle allows you to hold the knife like a pen. The rounded blade and long bevel act like a wedge and part the wood while you incise the line, which allows the darkening compound to fill the cut more easily. The arc in the blade also allows you to make graceful curves.

MATERIALS:

- 6¼" (160mm) circular basswood plate or material of choice
- Graphite paper
- Finely ground or instant coffee
- Oil finish of choice
- Beeswax, thinned-down polyurethane varnish, or wax finish of choice

Materials & Tools

- Soft paper towels
- Assorted sandpaper up to 600 grit
- Spray bottle of water or rubbing alcohol

TOOLS:

- Kolrosing knife
- Paintbrush of choice (to apply oil and finish)

SPECIAL SOURCES:

Judy and Del Stubbs of Pinewood Forge worked together to replicate the knives originally made by the late Ragnavald Froysadal. Judy also has a video on kolrosing available. **www.Pinewoodforge.com** or **800-423-1844**.

Carving a Snowman Collector's Plate

By Robert Biermann

This cheery snowman is an intaglio carving. Where traditional relief carving removes the background so the subject stands proud, intaglio carving recesses the main subject below the surrounding background. Both carving styles use similar techniques and can use the same pattern, but they produce distinctly different results.

Begin with a 10" (240mm)-diameter flat beaded plate, available from most woodcarving suppliers. Start by cutting out the pattern and placing it on the plate with the grain running parallel to the fence. Slide a piece of graphite paper under the pattern and trace along the pattern lines to transfer the design. I don't use carbon paper because it smears and is hard to erase.

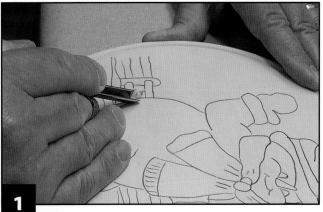

1

Define the elements. Position a 6mm (¼") #15 V-tool with the outside wing of the *V* perpendicular to the plate. The outside of the cut is vertical. Cut around the perimeter of the snowman, broom, fence, ground, and snow. Do not use the V-tool on the face. Use a knife to make a deep stop cut along the perpendicular edge. Keep the edge clean and smooth.

2

Round and lower the body. Use a 10mm (⅜") #3 gouge. Think of the snowman as being carved in the round. Round the edges to create depth and perspective. Continue lowering and rounding the body, separating the elements so you can begin to see the shape. One of the snowman's legs is behind the other and should be carved slightly deeper.

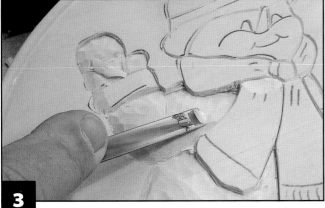

3 Shape the snowman's right arm. Lower and round the arm to create depth. Envision the carving in the round and taper the arm down so the shoulder appears to go under the scarf. Remove less wood from the forearm and mitten, which are closest to the surface, so they look closest to the viewer.

4 Round the face. Stop-cut along the hat brim with a knife. Use an 8mm (⁵⁄₁₆") #3 gouge to round the face, removing more wood from the left side. Outline the nose with a 6mm (¼") #15 V-tool. Slant the V-tool's wings toward the nose, but do not undercut. The tip of the nose is higher than the base, but lower than the hat brim.

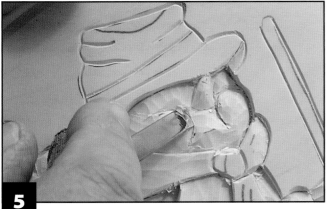

5 Round the cheeks and mouth. Use an 8mm (⁵⁄₁₆") #3 gouge. Turn the gouge upside down and press it in along the cheek line. Maintain the same arc as you shape the rest of the cheeks. Form the mouth barrel. Do not carve the eyes or mouth, but pencil them in to gauge their shape and position. Use an 8mm (⁵⁄₁₆") #3 gouge to shape the left hand, which is the lowest part of the snowman.

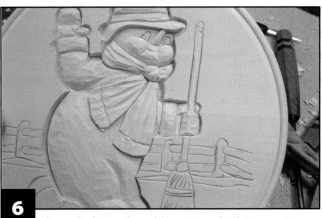

6 Shape the hat and scarf. Use an 8mm (⁵⁄₁₆") #3 gouge to round the edges of the scarf and lower the ends so it appears to go around the neck. Round the hat and undercut the brim slightly. Carve the folds in the hat and scarf. Deepen the stop cuts around the edges to produce shadows. The shadows at the face and back side of the body are stronger than the shadow at the right foot.

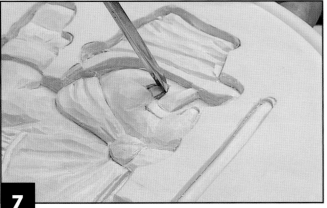

7 Carve the eyes. Match the sweep of a gouge, such as a 4mm (³⁄₁₆") #9, to the curve at the top of the eye. Position the tool on the line and angle the handle so the bevel is vertical. Press lightly to make a shallow cut. Complete the outline of the eye with a knife. Hold the knife at a low angle and cut a small chip around the eyeball. Shave and round the eye. Repeat the process on the other eye.

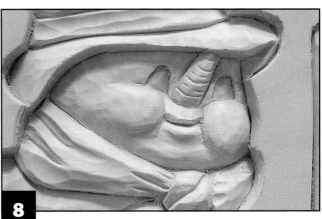

8 Carve the face details. Make a stop cut along the mouth with a knife. Hold the knife vertical to keep from chipping the lip. Shave wood from the top of the lower lip. Cut under the lower lip with a 4mm (³⁄₁₆") #9 gouge to make the chin. Add the carrot texture. Make sure the scarf knot is realistic and add the fringe. The folds in the hat and scarf are smooth and flowing.

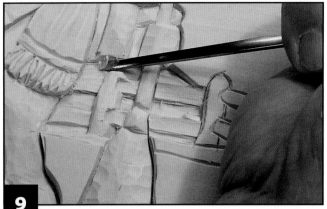

9 **Carve the fence and broom.** Lower the fence posts and rails so they are deeper than the snowman. Go deep enough so they appear to be behind the snowman. Carve the intersection of the posts and rails so it looks like the rails sit on the posts. Round the poles and rails. Shape the broom and reduce the thickness of the broomstick so it appears to go into the snowman's left hand.

10 **Add texture and shadows.** Add lines simulating grain to the fence posts and rails with a 2mm (1/16") #11 gouge. Add texture to the glove cuffs and broom straw with a 3mm (1/8") #15 V-tool. Texture the snow mounds behind the snowman with an 8mm (5/16") #3 gouge. Clean up all of the vertical cut edges and deepen the cuts slightly with a knife. Do not undercut. Remove any remaining fuzzies.

11 **Prepare for paint.** Liberally coat the entire plate with boiled linseed oil. Be sure the cuts are covered all of the way to the bottom. Remove excess oil with a paper towel. Oily towels are a fire hazard; dispose of them properly. Allow the plate to dry overnight. Apply several light coats of clear matte finish, buffing the surface lightly with a crumbled paper bag between coats.

12 **Apply the base coat.** Thin acrylic paints with clear wood stain. This method reduces runs and makes it easier to blend colors. Keep the stain in a small cup and add drops of paint to your palette. Pick up stain with a brush and mix it with the paint. Apply light coats, applying color heaviest in the shadowed areas. Add more stain to the paint, blending to almost no color in the center.

13 **Paint the snowman.** Use undiluted black paint for the pupils and eyebrows. Add a thin strip of blue heaven for the irises. Use a toothpick to add a light ivory highlight to each eye. Shade the cheeks and lips with light coats of thinned cadmium red. Thin blue heaven with stain and highlight the shadows of the snow, including the snowman's body and the snow in the background.

14 **Add shading and highlighting.** Blend the paint out from the shadows. Dry brush burnt umber on the fence. Darken the grooves in the broom with burnt umber. Dry brush light ivory on the scarf, hat band, and fence top. Use a toothpick to add dots of undiluted light ivory on the scarf and hat band. Apply two coats of matte sealer. Buff between coats with the crumbled paper bag.

© 2011 Woodcarving Illustrated

MATERIALS:

- 10" (240mm)-diameter flat beaded plate
- Boiled linseed oil
- Clear matte finish
- Water-based wood stain, decorator tint formula
- Palette paper or freezer paper
- Brown paper bag (without ink or printing)

- Acrylic paints:
  Light ivory (snow, broom lacing)
  Brown velvet (fence and broomstick)
  Burnt sienna (hat, gloves, scarf fringe)
  Orange (nose)
  Black (eyes)
  Blue heaven (eyes, shadows on snow)
  Burnt umber (fence and broom texture)
  Larkspur blue (scarf and hat band)
  Primary yellow (broom straw)
  Cadmium red (cheek highlights)
  Midnight (scarf highlights)

Materials & Tools

TOOLS:

- Carving knife of choice
- 2mm (¹⁄₁₆") #11 gouge
- #3 gouges: 3mm (⅛"), 5mm (³⁄₁₆"), 8mm (⁵⁄₁₆"), 10 mm (⅜")
- 4mm (³⁄₁₆") #9 gouge
- #15 45° V-tools: 3mm (⅛"), 6mm (¼")
- Paintbrushes of choice

Note: References to tool sizes and types refer to Pfiel designations.

Relief Carve an Autumn Scene

By Robert Biermann

This landscape is technically an intaglio carving because the carving is lower than the background, but it does have more of a traditional relief carving appearance.

The three main levels in this design are the background, the barn, and the limbs and leaves in the foreground. However, as with a carving depicting a face, areas within any given level are carved to different depths to create the proper perspective. If a face is turned to one side, the side farthest from the viewer will be deeper than the other side. The back side of the barn and roof, where the shed is attached, is deeper than the front side.

Carving

I start with a flat beaded 10"-diameter plate. Orient the plate so the grain runs from left to right and transfer the pattern to the plate with carbon paper. Carve along all of the lines with a 6mm 45° V-tool. Along the perimeter, where the design borders uncarved wood, keep the outside wing of the V-tool perpendicular to the surface of the wood. Use the V-tool normally for the other lines.

Once the elements are defined, remove the wood from the deepest parts of the scene. I use a drill bit with a stop collar to remove excess wood and clean up the drill marks with a #3 gouge. Use the same technique to remove wood from the middle level. Once the levels are blocked out, you can go back and carve the details and texture. Work hard to get the proper perspective in the carving.

Painting

Remove all fuzzies and chatter marks from dull tools. Make sure you have a stop cut where one object meets another. Then apply a coat of undiluted boiled linseed oil and wipe off the oil with paper towels. Spread out the oily towels in a well-ventilated area to dry. Oil-soaked towels can spontaneously combust. Allow the carving to dry overnight. Apply thinned washes of paint to the carving. Build up the color with repeated coats to get the coverage you desire. Then shade the areas that should be darker, such as the leaves, mountain, and side of the barn. After the paint dries, seal the carving with clear matte finish.

Materials & Tools

MATERIALS:
- 10" (240mm)-diameter flat beaded basswood plate
- Acrylic paints:
  Blue heaven (sky)
  Payne's gray (mountain)
  Antique white (mountain)
  Brown velvet (trees and fence)
  Burnt sienna (roof)
  Black green (shading)
  Buttermilk (mountain)
  Primary yellow (leaves)
  Burnt orange (leaves)
  Plantation pine (leaves)
  Heritage brick (silo)
  Midnight blue (shading)
  Barnwood (barn and shed)
  Light gray (shading)

TOOLS:
- V-tools of choice
- #3 gouges: assorted sizes from 2mm to 10mm
- 6mm (¼") #7 or #8 gouge
- 3mm or 4mm (⅛" or ³⁄₁₆") #11 veiner
- Knife

Photocopy at 100%

Relief Carve a
Magical Fairy Door

By Christina White

These whimsical doors are ideal for beginners or experienced carvers looking for a break from larger projects. Young children will enjoy adding the brightly painted finish, and older children can carve their very own doors. Carve several doors in advance and have a painting party!

The idea of a fairy door is far from new, but the variations of details, colors, and themes can go on forever. I have never done two alike. The doors can look like a miniature version of your house door, be hobbit-like, or have unique details, as if the fairies built them from objects they found lying about.

The fun inspired by these little fairy doors is more than I ever imagined, and I hope to pass on my enthusiasm. Children love them and the stories that naturally come about from seeing them are wonderful. Without fairies about, everything would go amok! Make them welcome.

Place the finished fairy door on the floor next to a door, tucked into a stairwell, along the baseboard, or on a shelf. The doors make delightful additions to a flower garden or front porch. Part of the charm is tucking them somewhere unexpected.

1 **Stop-cut around the elements in the carving.** Transfer the pattern to the blank. Stop-cut around the highest levels, which are the shaded areas on the pattern. Use a ⁵⁄₁₆" (8mm) straight chisel. Do not carve the top triangle on the main roof as it must remain flat to attach the overhanging roof.

2 **Rough out the door.** Cut close to the stop cut with a 60° ¼" (6mm) V-tool. This cut protects the stop cut edges as you remove ¼" (6mm) of wood from the door and wall with a ⁵⁄₁₆" (8mm) #5 gouge. Leave the surface rough, as we will be texturing these areas later.

3 **Rough out the overhanging roof.** Use the same technique to stop cut, separate the elements, and lower the siding area on the overhanging roof. Use a ⁵⁄₃₂" (4mm) #8 gouge to remove ¼" (6mm) of wood.

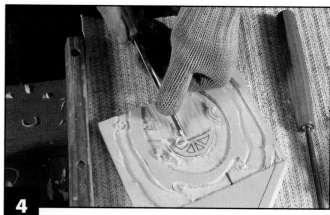

4 **Add texture to the door.** Make a series of vertical grooves with a ⁵⁄₃₂" (4mm) #8 gouge. Do not carve into the window, hinges, or handle. Clean up any rough edges near the corners of the door with a knife or 60° ¼" (6mm) V-tool.

5 **Carve the siding, shingles, and door boards.** Use the pattern as a guide to sketch in the shingles on the wall, the siding on the overhanging roof, and the vertical boards on the door. Carve along these lines with a 60° ¼" (6mm) V-tool.

6 **Undercut the siding and shingles.** Taper the siding on the overhanging roof to create the effect of the top board overlapping the board below it. Use a ⁵⁄₁₆" (8mm) #5 gouge. Use the same gouge to taper the shingles. The paint or stain you apply later will highlight the texture left by the gouge and add to the rustic appearance.

MATERIALS:

- 1" x 6" x 11" (25mm x 150mm x 280mm) basswood or white pine (main door and overhanging roof)
- Gouache paints (or paints of choice): Primary red Primary blue Yellow
- Boiled linseed oil mixed with burnt sienna or burnt umber oil paint

Materials & Tools

TOOLS:

- 5⁄16" (8mm) straight chisel
- 5⁄16" (8mm) skew chisel
- 5⁄16" (8mm) #5 gouge
- 5⁄32" (4mm) #8 gouge
- 60° ¼" (6mm) V-tool
- Carving knife

Carve the front gable (outlined in red) separately and mount it on the base carving.

© 2011 Woodcarving Illustrated

www.woodcarvingillustrated.com/patterns/relief-carve-a-magical-fairy-door.html

Photocopy at 100%

7 **Round the log elements.** Use a ⁵⁄₁₆" (8mm) #5 gouge to round the edges of the overhang, the door frame, and the logs supporting the overhang. Then carve along the roof line on the main blank with a 60° ¼" (6mm) V-tool. Round the edges of the roof back to this groove with a ⁵⁄₁₆" (8mm) #5 gouge.

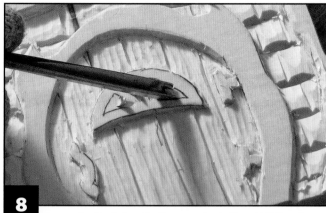

8 **Carve the final details.** Use a carving knife or ⁵⁄₁₆" (8mm) skew chisel to carve the door handle and hinges. Use the same tool to carve the windows on the door and the overhanging roof.

9 **Glue the pieces together.** Glue and clamp the roof overhang to the main blank. Leave about ¾" (20mm) of the top of the main blank exposed to show the front of both roof lines.

10 **Paint the door.** I use water-based gouache paints. Use your paint and colors of choice. Try to leave a little bit of space between the colors so they don't bleed when you add the oil finish. The oil finish will subdue the bright colors.

11 **Finish the door.** Mix burnt sienna or burnt umber oil paint with boiled linseed oil. Use a small natural-hair brush to apply the oil mixture to the carving. Allow the oil to soak in and then wipe off the excess. Dispose of oil-soaked rags or paper towels properly.

Bulldog Bulletin Board

By Kathy Wise

Look at this bulletin board in the morning, and you'll start your day with a bull-doggish attitude—ready to take on the world while taking no guff. I'll show you how to carve and shape the dog, the board, the bone stickpins, and a frame that matches the bulldog's collar. The second part will cover how to stain and finish your bulldog bulletin board.

I hope you enjoy carving your bulldog as much as I did designing, sculpting, and creating it!

Materials & Tools

Materials:
- 2" x 12" x 24" (50mm x 300mm x 600mm) basswood
- ¼" x 6" x 6" (6mm x 150mm x 150mm) white ash
- 4 each, white bulletin board pins
- ¼"- and ⁵⁄₁₆" (6mm and 8mm)- diameter dowels
- Roll of clear shelf contact paper
- Spray adhesive
- Yellow wood glue
- Carbon paper
- Razor blades or craft knife
- ¼" (6mm)-thick rolled cork

Tools:
- Scroll saw with #5 blade
- Table saw
- Power drill with ¼"- and ⁵⁄₁₆" (6mm and 8mm)-diameter bits
- Handheld rotary tool ½" (13mm) sanding band
- Assorted grinding bits
- Flap wheel
- Assorted carving tools

1 **Copy the pattern and use spray adhesive to apply it to the contact paper,** which keeps the pattern from shifting. Peel off the back and apply it to the wood. Use a scroll saw to cut out the bulldog's outline. Use a table saw to cut the straight edges of the spiked frame. Do not cut out the inside box yet.

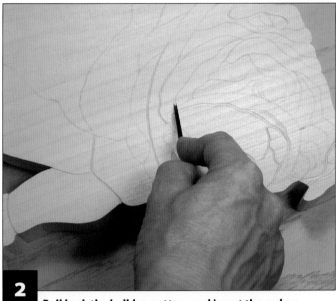

2 **Pull back the bulldog pattern and insert the carbon paper.** Trace the pattern onto the wood, pressing hard. Begin by carving the lines that have been traced with a V-tool or small gouge.

3 **Use gouges to cut under the feet.** Carve the ears back, and shape under the collar, the belly, and tail. Gouge out the different levels.

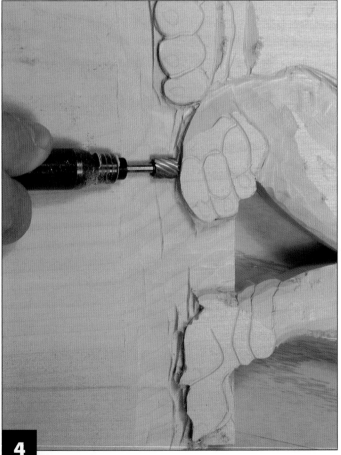

4 **If you prefer, use a grinder to quickly take wood off the edges of the piece,** under the collar, on the feet, and on the belly.

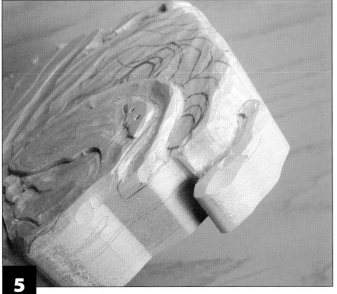

5 **Continue defining the shapes of each layer.** Go back in with gouges as needed. You want to create sculpted levels. Round the edges of the piece and retrace the face wrinkles after you carve the levels.

6 **Examine the bulldog from different angles** to determine where additional carving is needed prior to sanding.

7 **Cut out the inside of the square with a scroll saw.** Plane down this inside piece to ¾" (20mm) or using the pattern, simply cut out a square piece from a ¾" (20mm)-thick board. Fit and glue it inside the frame. Drill holes for the spikes in the collar and frame with ¼"- and ⁵⁄₁₆"-(6mm and 8mm) diameter drill bits.

8 **Make the spikes.** The five collar spikes are smaller than the 14 frame spikes. Use the ¼" (6mm)-diameter dowel for the collar and the ⁵⁄₁₆" (8mm)-diameter for the frame. Start with a 2'-long dowel so you can work safely. Insert the dowel into the hole and mark the desired height with a pencil. Remove the dowel and sharpen the point; you can use a knife or a power sander for a fast and efficient job. Flatten it slightly with a piece of fine sandpaper. Number each dowel to fit into the hole you measured it for to ensure the correct depth; some holes may have been drilled deeper than others. Repeat for the frame spikes.

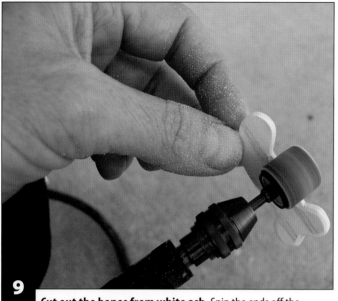

9 **Cut out the bones from white ash.** Snip the ends off the bulletin board pins with wire cutters. Round the edges of the bones. I used the grinder because ash is very hard. Glue the pins to the bones with epoxy.

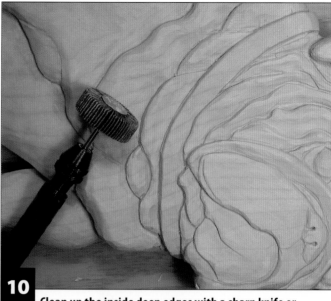

10 **Clean up the inside deep edges with a sharp knife or craft knife.** This makes the piece look neater, and the cuts also help prevent the stain from bleeding. Do any hand sanding needed. I used a small flap wheel to sand most parts.

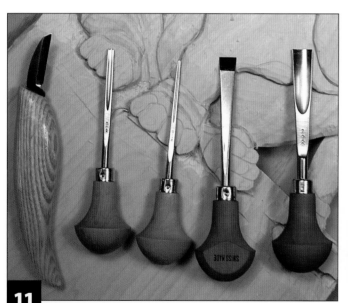

11 **I used a variety of tools, from hand gouges to carving and craft knives to grinding tools.** Some of my favorites are pictured above: a carving knife, #11 3mm (⅛"), #11 1mm (¹⁄₃₂"), #1 12mm (½") and #7 14mm (⅝") palm gouges. Use whatever tools you feel comfortable working with; it is the end result that counts.

12 **Check the entire piece** and make sure you are satisfied with the carving and finish sanding.

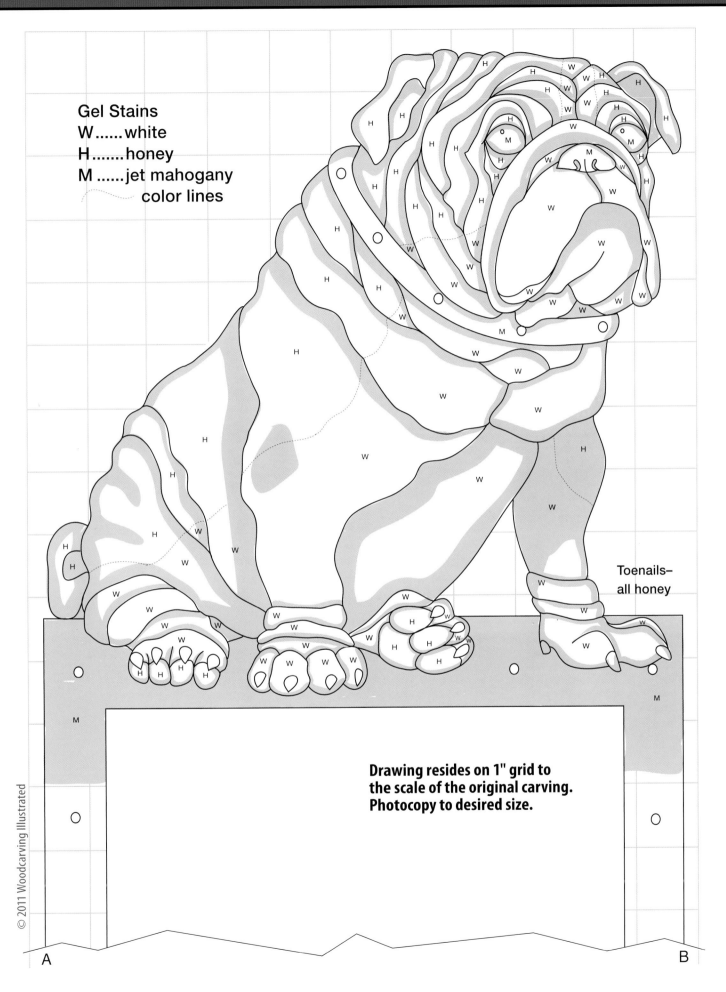

Gel Stains
W ......white
H ....honey
M ......jet mahogany
         color lines

Toenails–
all honey

**Drawing resides on 1" grid to
the scale of the original carving.
Photocopy to desired size.**

© 2011 Woodcarving Illustrated

A   B

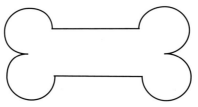

Dog Bone Stick Pin Pattern

Photocopy at 100%

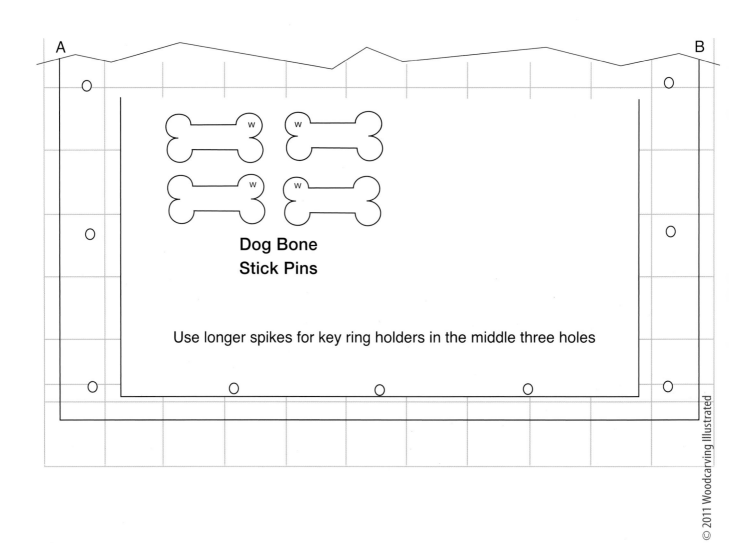

A   B

Dog Bone
Stick Pins

Use longer spikes for key ring holders in the middle three holes

Finishing the Bulldog Bulletin Board

By Kathy Wise

Now that you have finished carving the bulldog project, I'll show you how to proceed with the finishing phase. You can make this bulldog any color you wish, maybe even match the colors of your pet or favorite mascot.

I finished mine in two colors, using a mixed honey gel stain and white base tint. For an eye-pleasing contrast I painted the collar and frame a dark jet mahogany. Spray-painted silver spikes studded along the collar and frame make this a very interesting piece. The unique stickpin bones add a whimsical quality that dog lovers will enjoy!

I hope you have fun working on the finishing stage of your bulldog bulletin board. With a little creativity you can make your project a one-of-a-kind piece of art.

MATERIALS:
- Carved Bulldog Bulletin Board
- 4 each, white stickpins
- Yellow wood glue
- Gel natural varnish
- Honey gel stain
- White base gel stain
- Jet mahogany gel stain
- Silver spray paint
- Modeling clay
- Wiping rags
- Paint thinner

Materials & Tools
- Sawtooth hanger
- Sandpaper, 220 grit
- Razor blades
- ¼" (6mm)-thick rolled cork, 12" x 12" (300mm x 300mm)
- Assorted small flat and round paintbrushes

TOOLS:
- Craft knife

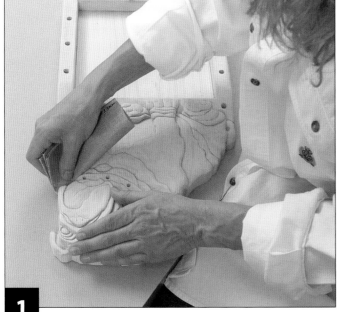

1   **Take another pass with 220-grit sandpaper** to ensure a smooth, blemish-free surface. Before you pick up a brush or open a can of stain, make sure you have your color scheme planned. Also consider where you want to put the highlights and shadows, though you should be ready and willing to make changes on the fly.

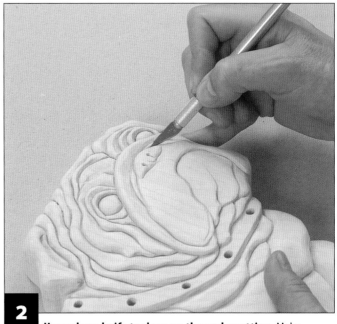

2   **Use a sharp knife to clean up the undercutting.** Make nice sharp cuts; they are more attractive, and the cut will keep the stains from bleeding.

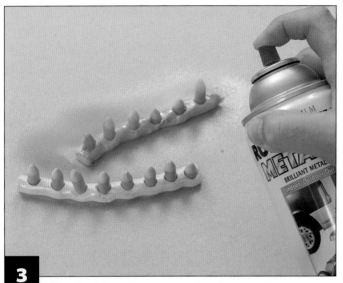

3 **After all of the spikes are completed, spray paint them.** To make quick work of this task, I insert the spikes in some modeling clay, which I've rolled out. A few passes with the silver spray paint and the spikes are completed. Let dry overnight.

CHECK YOUR WORK   **TIP**

As you're working, stop every so often to view the piece from a distance so you can see how your accents, highlights, and shadows are working.

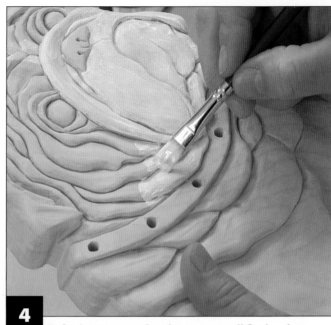

4 **Referring to your color plan, use a small flat brush to apply one coat of the white gel stain** to the white areas. Cover all of the areas you want to be white completely; if you don't, the finish coat of varnish will turn uncovered areas a dull yellow. Let the stain soak in a minute or two. Carefully wipe it away with a clean cotton rag.

Be careful not to get the white gel stain on non-white areas of the project. To keep from dragging stain into an unintended area, get in the habit of turning to a clean area of the rag after every wipe.

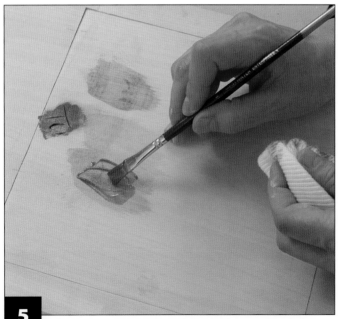

5 **The color shown on the honey stain can looked to be about right.** However, when I did a test on the back of the project, it appeared too dark for my liking. To tone down the color, I simply mixed it with a little of the clear varnish. If you don't want to do your mixing on the back of the bulletin board as I've done, make sure you test on the same wood you used for your project. Testing on the back of the actual project adds a certain level of authenticity to the project that a potential buyer may find appealing.

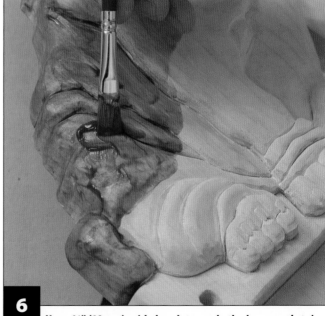

6 **Use a ⅜" (10mm)-wide brush to apply the honey gel stain** to the back and each side of the head following the marking on the pattern. Let it soak in a minute or two, then wipe the stain away again with the clean rag. Always wipe **away** from the white area, not toward it. Don't worry about getting it near or on the carved parts of the eyes or nose; darker colors added later will cover any mistakes. Thin down the honey stain even more with the gel varnish and darken the cut lines along the wrinkles in the white area to bring out the sculpted aspects of the dog.

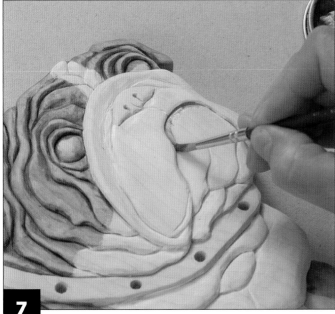

7 Using a detail brush, apply the thinned-down honey and jet mahogany gel stain mix under the mouth and around the nose area to give the illusion of shadow areas. Make sure you get it in the cracks and the areas you want but not beyond. You won't be able to get the dark color out of the light area. Gently dab away the excess stain.

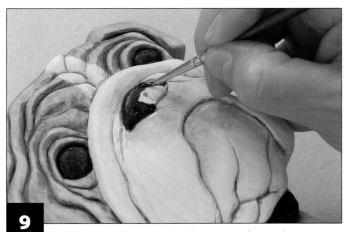

9 Dab the jet mahogany onto the eyes and nose. Do not wipe or brush the stain. Using a rag, dab the center of the eyes and nose to remove the excess stain. Turn the rag to a clean side each time.

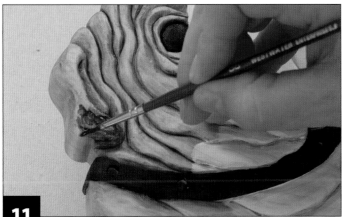

11 Continue adding the darker accent details with the detail brush to the tips of the ears, the lips, and jowls. Dab off with a clean rag.

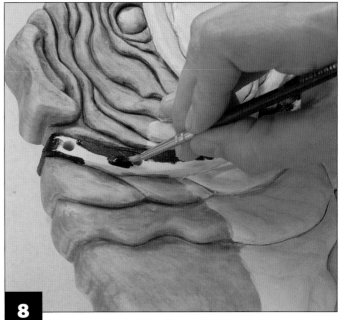

8 Using a small detail brush, carefully brush the jet mahogany gel stain onto the collar. Do not get any on the rest of the dog or you will have a spotted bulldog; the dark color will not come out of a light area.

10 Use a detail brush to paint the frame background color around the toes. Continue using the dark color to complete the frame. Make sure the mahogany color goes in the holes so no bare wood shows after the spikes are inserted. I paint the frame from the top down so I don't need to worry about getting my fingers in the stain and contaminating other areas of the project.

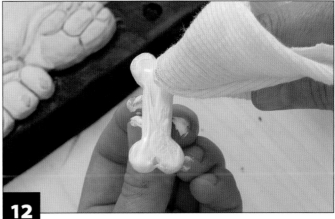

12 Glue the stickpins to the bones with epoxy. Let dry overnight. Apply the white color to the bones with a brush and let set for five minutes. Wipe it away with a clean rag and let dry overnight. Apply clear gel varnish and let dry overnight.

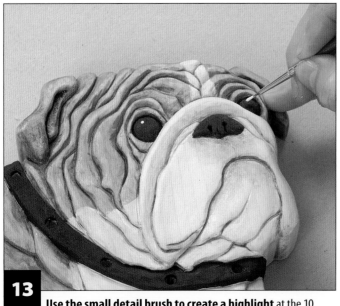

13 **Use the small detail brush to create a highlight** at the 10 o'clock position on each eye. I used white oil base paint for this detail. Let the stained project dry overnight.

14 **Put a little yellow woodworking glue into each of the holes** you have drilled for the spikes. Insert the spikes into their numbered holes. You may have to taper each one slightly to fit easily.

15 **Cut and fit ¼" (6mm)-thick cork into the frame.** Leave a little extra to trim down for a tight and attractive fit. Glue with yellow woodworking glue and weigh it down. I use the stain cans with the extra weight on top after I put a piece of plastic down first to ensure that any spills of stain do not get on the project. Let the entire piece dry overnight before applying a clear gel varnish as the finishing touch. Once it is dry, add the bone stickpins and sawtooth hanger.

16 **Your Bulldog Bulletin Board is complete and ready to hang!**

Country Charm Quilt Squares

By Lora S. Irish

These simple relief designs, which can be carved in one day with just a few tools and supplies, are ideal for new carvers.

The project can easily be adapted to any number of patterns or designs. Add a piece of corkboard for a message center, incorporate the design into a sign, carve several different patterns and join them together for a carved quilt, or carve individual squares to be displayed on their own or as a group.

My instructions focus on carving the design with a corkboard overlay for use as a message center.

Adding a bark frame and corkboard creates a handy message board.

1 **Transfer the pattern to the blank.** Sand the wood smooth, and remove the dust. Center the pattern in the top section and transfer to the blank with carbon paper. Open a compass ¾" (19mm) wide. With the point leg over the edge of the board and the pencil leg on the face, make a reference line for the border. Use a ruler and pencil to mark a line 8½" (220mm) from the top.

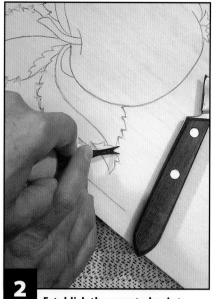

2 **Establish the serrated points in the leaves.** Push a large V-tool into the wood to make stop cuts around the edges of the leaves. The V-tool profile creates identical serrations and gives the leaf edges an even, balanced look.

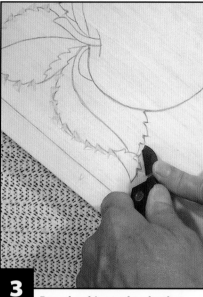

3 **Free the chips and make the remaining stop cuts.** Cut the chips around the leaves free with a bench knife or chip carving knife. Hold the knife perpendicular to the blank, and cut around the remaining elements. Re-cut this stop cut line angling the knife slightly away from the design. This will release a thin slice of wood.

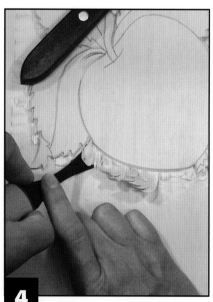

4 **Remove the background wood.** Use a wide-sweep gouge and a large, round gouge interchangeably. Cut up to the stop cut you created in step 3. Repeat steps 2 through 4 until you have worked the background down to your desired depth (mine is ⅜" (10mm) deep). Slope your cuts so they create a bowl shape that is shallow along the reference lines and deepest at the pattern lines.

5 **Establish the different levels of the leaves.** Mark arrows on the wood where you want to drop the leaf area deeper. I drop the inside of the leaf under the apple and taper the outside toward the center leaf vein. Cut the center vein with a V-tool. Taper the sections with a wide-sweep gouge or a bull-nose chisel. You are only establishing the depth, not shaping these areas.

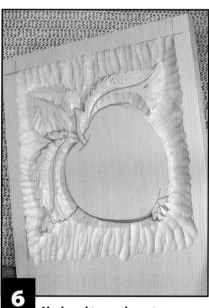

6 **Mark and taper the outer edges of the leaves.** Mark the direction of the taper with a pencil. Then taper the wood with a wide-sweep gouge or bull-nose chisel.

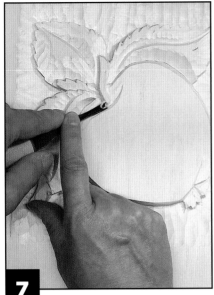

7 **Establish the apple stem and the dimple at the top of the apple.** Use a V-tool. Then move on to the bottom of the apple—the blossom area. Use a V-tool to carve the separation line between the blossom and apple. Then taper the blossom below the apple surface with a wide-sweep gouge.

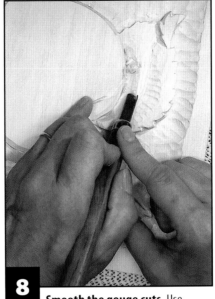

8 **Smooth the gouge cuts.** Use a bull-nose chisel. You can also use a straight chisel, a skew chisel, or a large, round gouge. Shape the curves of the leaves, the stems, and the blossom area. The goal is to create the shape and smooth away the rough ridges without losing the carved look. Leave some of the texture of the cut strokes.

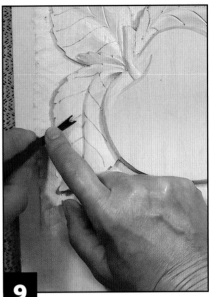

9 **Add the small side veins.** Mark the veins with a pencil, and cut along the pencil lines with a V-tool. Follow the contour of the leaves as you make the vein cut.

10 **Round the edges of the apple.** Use a wide-sweep gouge or bull-nose chisel. Drop the area of the apple down behind the stem slightly so it's deeper than the stem. Use a wide-sweep gouge to taper the bottom half of the apple toward the blossom area. The center of the apple is the highest point of the carving. Make a few shallow strokes across this area to match the texture of the rest of the carving.

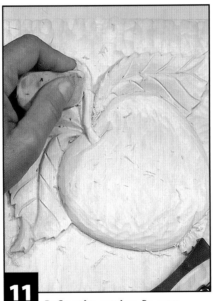

11 **Refine the carving.** Re-carve any area that seems rough. Clean up the edge lines with a bench knife, and smooth the joint lines. In essence, repeat all the steps as needed to give the piece a finished shape and smooth look. Remove chips and fibers with an old toothbrush. Use a white artist's eraser to remove pencil lines, soil marks, carbon paper lines, and any loose fibers. Remove the dust.

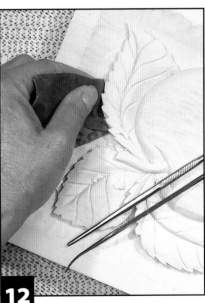

12 **Add undercuts (optional).** For more depth, add undercuts to the outer edges of the leaves. Make an angled stop cut under the leaves with a chip carving or bench knife. Then cut along the background to meet up with the first cut. This removes a V-shaped sliver of wood from under the leaf's edge. Clean up the cuts with sandpaper, a dental tool, or a riffler. I undercut the blossom area, but not the apple itself.

Creating a message center

Cut corkboard the same size as the board. Make a line 1" (25mm) and 8" (200mm) down from the top and 1" (25mm) in from both sides. Cut this section out so the carving shows through. Apply an even coat of wood glue to the uncarved areas of the blank. Position the cork over the carving, place a sheet of wax paper over the corkboard, and clamp securely until dry. Use scrap wood to avoid clamp marks on the cork.

Remove the clamps. Cut away the excess corkboard along the edge of the carving with a wide-sweep gouge. Let the gouge cuts continue into the basswood background area to unite the two surfaces.

The frame edge of the project is red cedar bark. Soak the bark in water for 2 to 3 minutes to make it pliable. Cut a strip of bark 3" (75mm) longer than the outside dimensions of your board and ¼" (6mm) wider than its thickness. Apply wood glue to the outer edge of the carving, and secure the bark to the edge with small brads. Allow the bark to overlap 3" (75mm) on the bottom edge. Clamp the bark with scrap boards until the glue has set.

Remove the clamps and apply two coats of polyurethane satin finish to the carved area only. Allow the corkboard and cedar bark to remain natural. Add a hanger to the back of the project.

Photocopy at 100% or desired size

© 2011 Woodcarving Illustrated

Materials & Tools

MATERIALS:
- ¾" x 8½" x 11" (19mm x 220mm x 280mm) basswood
- ⅛" x 8½" x 11" (3mm x 220mm x 280mm) corkboard sheeting
- Sandpaper, 220 grit
- Masking tape
- Carbon paper
- Satin polyurethane finish
- Wood glue
- ⅛" (3mm) red cedar bark strip long enough to go around the carving and overlap 3" (76mm)

- Hardware hanger

TOOLS:
- Compass
- Bench knife or large chip carving knife
- V-tool
- Wide sweep gouge and/or large round gouge
- Bullnose chisel
- Toothbrush or stiff dusting brush
- White artist's eraser

Hen Board

By Lora S. Irish

I was carving the hen board and really got carried away with the detailing. I had meant the piece to be a simple, fairly smooth, folk-art-style piece but, as always, just had to fuss it up a bit...a real big bit. I added color to make the design stand out.

Because this is carved on ¾" (20mm)-thick basswood, the layer work is quite shallow between the individual levels. Carve just enough from each area to tuck it under the adjacent area. The layers pattern shows the design worked with the highest layer in the palest tone and lower layers in darker tones.

The deepest carved areas of the project, the spaces between the wood slats in the nesting box, are about ½" (13mm) deep. For the highest areas, I simply rolled over along the edge of the area, then detailed. One area of the design, the wheat stalk under the hen's eggs, tapers from the highest layer near the eggs to the level of the rooster's back tail feathers.

■ **Level 1 (lowest layer)**

■ **Level 2**

▨ **Level 3**

▨ **Level 4**

□ **Level 5 (highest layer)**

Photocopy at 130% or desired size

Relief Carve a
Winter Lighthouse

By Robert Stadtlander

Lighthouses make great relief scenes. This particular scene captures the bright warmth of the lighthouse in contrast with the cold winter night. The project provides many hours of carving fun and employs a few special techniques to enhance your relief carvings. This derivative work is based on a painting by Jesse Barnes and is reproduced with his permission.

I use an oval basswood blank, but other board shapes can be used as well. Use a nonslip pad to secure the piece as you carve.

Start by transferring the pattern to the blank. Draw a horizontal centerline across your blank. Tape a copy of the pattern to the blank with masking tape and slip a piece of carbon paper between the blank and the pattern. Slide the carbon paper around as you trace the lines with a red ballpoint pen. Use the water's horizon and the base of the shrubs in front of the house as guides to level the scene against the centerline. Omit the fine details when transferring the pattern to save time. Remove the pattern and carbon paper.

PRACTICE DIFFICULT SECTIONS   **TIP**

The trees are more difficult to carve than they look. Practice carving them on a scrap piece of wood first.

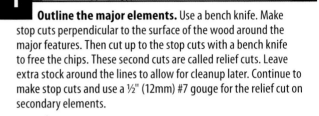

1 **Outline the major elements.** Use a bench knife. Make stop cuts perpendicular to the surface of the wood around the major features. Then cut up to the stop cuts with a bench knife to free the chips. These second cuts are called relief cuts. Leave extra stock around the lines to allow for cleanup later. Continue to make stop cuts and use a ½" (12mm) #7 gouge for the relief cut on secondary elements.

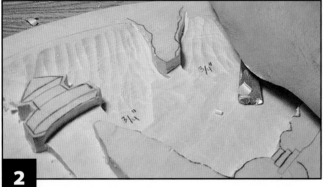

2 **Carve the background.** Use a ⁵⁄₁₆" (8mm) #8 gouge and ¼" (6mm) flat fishtail skew for the tight areas. Carve the sky down to a depth of ¾" (19mm) in the deepest areas. Recess the lighthouse back to a depth of ½" (13mm), then use wider #3 gouges to make this surface as flat as possible. Leave the railing of the lighthouse and chimney smoke raised. Clean up any leftover stop cuts using a #3 gouge.

3 **Carve the foreground.** Carve the trees and shrubs back to a depth of ¼" (6mm). Make an angled cut alongside the steps, but leave the steps raised. Draw the windows, door, and eaves. Use a straight edge wherever possible and make sure the two windows on each side of the door are the same width and height. Leave the eaves wide enough for the icicles. Draw the snow and icicles on top of the door.

4 **Break the major elements into the smaller components.** Carve the right side of the house ¹⁄₁₆" (2mm) deeper than the left side and redraw the right window. Leave the eaves, shutters, windows, and door raised by carving the wall ¹⁄₁₆" (2mm) deeper. Take the lighthouse cap and railing section down to ³⁄₈" (10mm). Carve the steps down ⅛" (3mm). Round the sides of the trees and draw the tree boughs.

5 **Carve the water and fence posts.** Carve around the lower rocks. Stop cut around the top of the large wave and use a ½" (13mm) #7 gouge to remove the wood below it. Remove wood around the fence posts except where they meet the ground. Carve the rocks on the cliff. Lower the large rock so the water appears to splash over it. Separate the fence posts from the railing with a ⅛" (3mm) V-tool. Round the posts with a #3 gouge.

6 **Shape the boughs.** Start at the top of the tree and work downward on one side. Make straight stop cuts on all of the bough lines. Repeat this process on the other side of the tree. Then make the relief cuts using a bench knife. Use a 5⁄16" (8mm) #8 gouge to carve some of the areas a little deeper. Make sure each bough has a continuous slope up to the bough above it. Lower the bushes an additional 1⁄16" (2 mm).

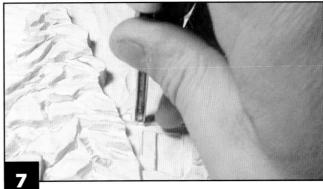

7 **Carve the house.** Carve the window panes 1⁄16" (2mm) deeper than the walls. Then flatten them with #3 gouges. Carve between the icicles with a 1⁄8" (3mm) U-gouge. Separate the snow on top of the door and lower the door. Lower the pillar of the lighthouse 1⁄8" (3mm) more between the railing and the house roof. Lower the railing area until it is 1⁄8" (3mm) above the pillar. Taper the house roof. The left and right peaks are deepest and are the same depth as the pillar.

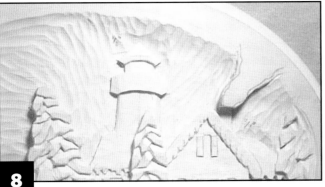

8 **Shape the lighthouse.** Taper the cap. Make a stop cut between the cap and the windows and deepen the windows. Round the lighthouse's sides. Taper the area below the railing to meet the pillar with a #3 gouge. This creates a bevel between the railing and the underside of the lighthouse. Use the same technique for the area under the cap. Shape the rocks lowering the bottoms to meet the water.

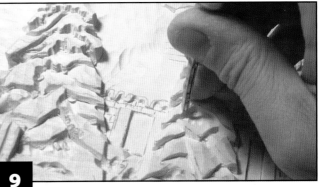

9 **Finish carving the trees.** Use a 5⁄8" (16mm) #3 gouge to angle the tip of each bough inward so it looks like snow weighs down the boughs. Drive 3⁄16", 1⁄8", and 1⁄16" (5mm, 3mm, and 2mm) U-gouges straight in on the bottom of each bough. Remove any chips with a toothbrush. Use a 5⁄16" (8mm) #8 gouge to taper the boughs in and under the boughs above them. Use a 1⁄8" (3mm) U-gouge to lightly texture the top of the boughs, but keep them relatively smooth to produce the look of snow.

10 **Carve the icicles and snow.** Use a 1⁄8" (3mm) V-tool to make cuts up toward the roof leaving the icicles pointed at the bottom. Make sure the icicles are random lengths. Round the top of the shrubs and pierce a few little holes in the front of the shrubs using 1⁄8" (3mm) and 1⁄16" (2mm) U-gouges. The shrubs are covered with snow, so don't add too much texture. Clean up any gouge marks on the house using #3 and skew gouges.

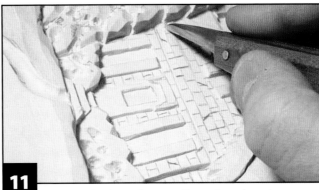

11 **Carve the bricks and stones.** Use a ruler to draw the horizontal lines spacing them about 3⁄16" (5mm) apart. Draw the vertical lines, staggering them from one row to the next. Alter a few stones by making some two rows high and making a few angled lines. Cut along the lines with a detail knife held at a 75° angle. Use a toothbrush to remove the chips. Round each stone with a detail knife and add texture to them with a shallow fishtail gouge.

12 **Finish carving the lighthouse.** Separate the stones on the sides of the lighthouse pillar with a 1⁄16" (2mm) V-tool. Draw in and carve the lighthouse window. Taper the left side of the chimney down to meet the sky. Draw in the chimney stones; the horizontal lines on the left side taper toward the back. Carve the bricks with a 1⁄16" (2mm) V-tool. Round the smoke and shape it with U-gouges. Make horizontal cuts to texture the smoke with a 1⁄8" (3mm) U-gouge.

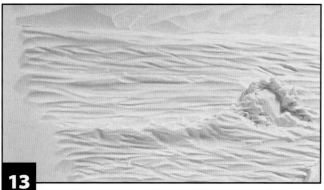

13 **Carve the water.** Round the top of the water near the horizon. Use 1⁄8" (3mm) and 1⁄16" (2mm) U-gouges to texture the water splashing over the large rock and along the top of the large wave. Use a 3⁄16" (5mm) U-gouge to carve horizontal lines in the water giving the appearance of swells. Repeat the process using 1⁄8" and 1⁄16" (3mm and 2mm) U-gouges to add additional texture. Vary the motion by angling the horizontal cuts, especially below the large wave.

14 **Finish carving the cliff and fence posts.** Texture the cliffs using a 1⁄8" (3mm) V-tool and a detail knife. Use a 1⁄16" (2mm) V-tool to separate the snow from the top of the fence posts and railings and use the same V-tool to carve the wood grain on the fence posts. Use a 1⁄16" (2mm) U-gouge to create a few knotholes by driving the gouge straight into the wood and popping out the chips.

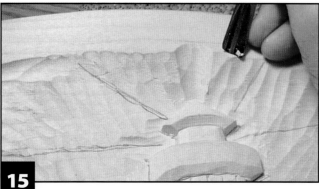

15 **Carve the path and light beams.** Use a 3⁄16" (5mm) U-gouge to carve the path. The path narrows as it approaches the door. Create snow drifts using a 1⁄2" (12mm) #7 gouge. Use a 1⁄2" (12mm) #5 gouge to texture the snow. Carve the steps with a 1⁄8" (3mm) flat gouge. The steps get progressively deeper toward the top. Trim the sides of the steps square. Draw lines starting from the lamp. Use a 1⁄2" (12mm) #7 gouge to make continuous grooves, leaving high ridges to simulate the light beams.

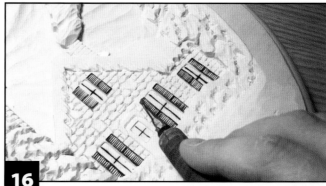

16 **Finish the carving.** Undercut around the roof, between the cliffs and water, and around the fence and trees. Sand the border, sides, and back. Flatten the area for the moon using a #3 gouge and draw it in. Draw the shutters and window panes. Woodburn the shutters, windows, doors, and railing. Use the side of a spear tip to shade the shutter frames and railing. Use the edge of the spear tip to separate the shutters and window panes.

Use scrap basswood to test the colors and consistency of the paint wash. Practice thoroughly blending the different colors.

17 **Apply a base coat.** Use a 20:1 (20 parts water to 1 part paint) mixture of water and French blue. Use a ½" (13mm)-wide flat brush to paint the sky and water, leaving the area around the light unpainted. Use a #6 shader brush for the small areas. Paint the undercuts and crevices. Dilute the wash with an additional 20 parts of water and paint the bricks, roof, snow, and smoke.

18 **Add darker shadows.** Use a 20:1 mixture of water and Payne's gray. While the base coat is wet, blend the Payne's gray wash into the dark sky areas near the border, around the top of the house and trees, and above the water horizon. Use the same wash to darken the deeper areas of the water and the shadows in the trees and shrubs.

19 **Paint the trees and details.** Use a 20:1 mixture of water with each color. Paint the trees and shrubs with Hooker's green. Use burnt umber for the door, fence posts and rails, and shadows on the trees and shrubs. Paint the rocks, cliff, chimney, shutters, lighthouse cap, under the railing, and window in the pillar with carbon black. Use the carbon black wash to add shadows to the trees, shrubs, under the icicles, and along the right side of the pillar.

20 **Paint the illuminated areas.** Use a 10:1 mixture of water and cadmium orange for the unpainted sky area, the windows, the railing, and the area where the light shines on the snow. Blend in the thinned Payne's gray and French blue when painting the snow. Use a 10:1 mixture of water and Indian yellow and apply it to the same areas. To avoid giving the sky a green tint, do not paint as far out with the yellow as you did with the orange.

21 **Paint the moon and moonlit areas.** Use a 10:1 mixture of water and Naples yellow to paint moonlight onto the background. Paint the moon with full-strength Naples yellow. Blend cadmium orange into the bottom of the moon and titanium white into the top of the moon. Let the paint dry. Apply a 50:50 mixture of water and titanium white where the moon reflects on the water. The reflection widens as it approaches the bottom of the scene.

22 **Highlight the snow and light areas.** Apply the titanium white mixture to the snow on the ground, fence posts, railings, trees, shrubs, roof, icicles, and left side of the lighthouse pillar. Then highlight the stones on the house and chimney, the chimney smoke, and the stones on the cliff. Blend some of this mixture into the sky between the orange and blue.

23 **Add the reflections and shadows.** Apply full-strength titanium white to the high spots on the water and the heavy snow on the trees and shrubs. Blend some Indian yellow and cadmium orange onto the trees and shrubs for the reflection of the light. Apply some of the thinned carbon black and thinned Payne's gray around the fence posts, pathway, and the bottom of the swells to add more shadows. Let the paint dry.

24 **Drybrush the carving.** Pick up a small amount of titanium white with a ½" (13mm)-diameter round brush. Remove most of the paint on a paper towel. Stroke the brush perpendicular to the raised areas on the crests of the waves, cliffs, stones on the buildings, chimney, smoke, trees, shrubs, fence posts, railings, and snow drifts.

25 **Finish the carving.** Paint the border and back with a 10:1 mixture of water and burnt umber. Allow the paint to dry for 72 hours and then seal the carving with water-based varnish. After the varnish dries, apply two or three coats of satin-finish polyurethane spray. Let the finish dry between coats. Wipe down the flat surfaces with a crumpled-up paper bag between coats.

MATERIALS:
- 1" x 14" x 18" (25mm x 360mm x 460mm) routed oval basswood board
- Lead pencil
- Large rubber eraser
- Carbon paper
- Masking tape
- Sandpaper: 60, 150, 240 grits
- Acrylic paints:
  French blue
  Hooker's green
  Burnt umber
  Carbon black
  Indian yellow
  Cadmium orange
  Titanium white
  Payne's gray
  Naples yellow
- Water-based varnish
- Satin-finish polyurethane spray

TOOLS:
- Nonslip pad
- Toothbrush
- 6"- and 12" (150mm and 300mm)-long rulers
- Carving glove
- Woodburner with spear tip
- Standard carving knife
- Detail bench knife

Materials & Tools

- ¼" (6mm) flat fishtail skew
- #3 long-bent gouges: ⅛", ⅜", ⅝" (3mm, 10mm, 16mm)
- ½" (12mm) #5 gouge
- ½" (12mm) # 7 gouge
- ⁵⁄₁₆" (8mm) #8 short-bent gouge
- ¹⁄₁₆" (2mm) U-gouge
- ⅛" (3mm) U-gouge
- ³⁄₁₆" (5mm) U-gouge
- ¹⁄₁₆" (2mm) V-tool
- ⅛" (3mm) V-tool
- Nylon brushes: ½" (13mm) flat, ½" (13mm) round, #6 shader

Oval basswood boards are available from www.stadtlandercarvings.com.

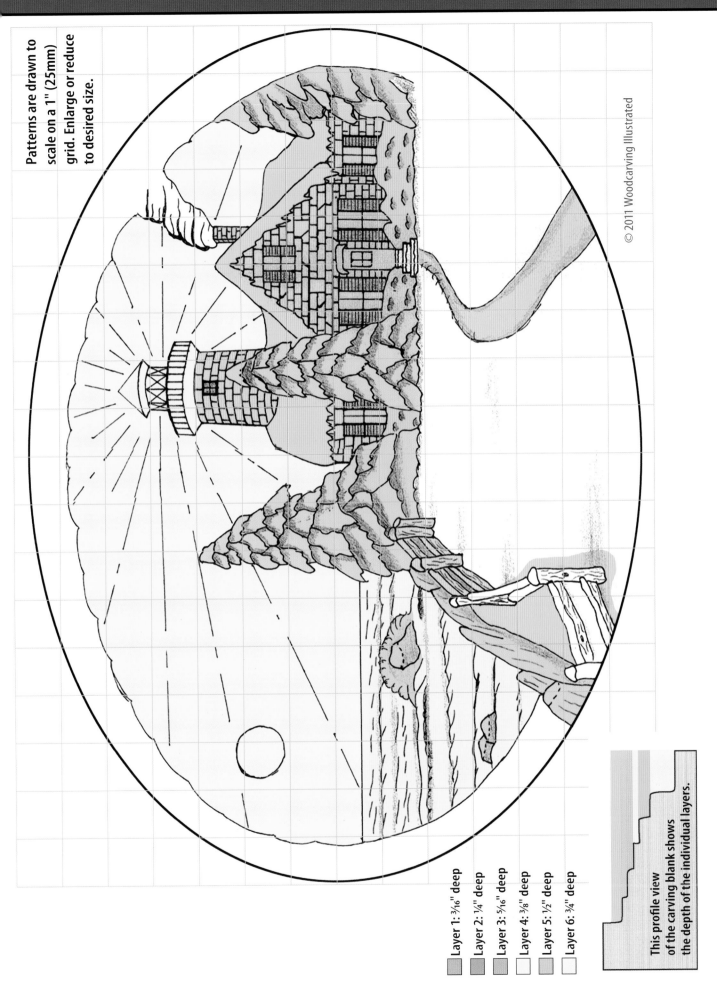

Patterns are drawn to scale on a 1" (25mm) grid. Enlarge or reduce to desired size.

Layer 1: $^3/_{16}$" deep
Layer 2: $^1/_4$" deep
Layer 3: $^5/_{16}$" deep
Layer 4: $^3/_8$" deep
Layer 5: $^1/_2$" deep
Layer 6: $^3/_4$" deep

This profile view of the carving blank shows the depth of the individual layers.

Color Guard

By Mary-Ann Jack-Bleach
Photos by Dennis Moor

1 **Prepare the blank.** Transfer the pattern to the blank. Cut the outline on a band saw, and attach it to ½" (13mm)-thick plywood with three 1" (25mm)-long screws from the back. Position the screws where you will not carve deeper than ¼" (6mm). Measure and mark the location of the screws with red dots on the blank. Attach the plywood to a carving vise.

Suggesting a three-dimensional form in thin wood can be difficult. Establishing correct proportions is key to creating the illusion. Don't carve the outside edges until the main carving is complete. This promotes a smoother transition and adds to the illusion of depth and dimension.

I designed this carving to accompany a display of my father's World War II medals. The carving is inspired by those who take care of us on a daily basis in law enforcement, fire and rescue, and the military, saving lives and even sacrificing their own lives in the course of duty.

Bernie Scheid, a constable in the London, Ontario, Police Force, who also served in the Canadian military, was my model for this carving.

I took photographs, including close-ups of his shoes, cap, and uniform, as Bernie simulated the stance. Use your own reference photos to change the uniform and flag design as desired. An alternate pattern depicting a woman in uniform is included.

The design is reasonably easy to carve and doesn't require facial details, which can be difficult for novice carvers to execute.

ROUGHING OUT | TIP

While carving, avoid getting so involved in the folds and creases that you remove too much wood. Remember, there are body parts under the uniform. Eliminate this risk by leaving an uncarved edge of ⅜" to ½" (10mm to 13mm) around the entire carving where it meets the plywood; carve the edge only during the final stages.

REFERENCE MATERIAL

Researching the subject matter while designing a carving is critical. I gained insight into my subject matter by taking the photographs myself and by talking to someone who has expert knowledge of different uniforms.

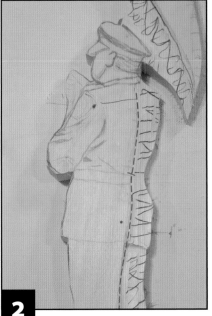

2 **Rough out the right side.** Mark the wood to be removed from the right side of the figure and inside the fold of the flag above the cap. The line indicates the midline of his back. Work from the center of the back down to the edge. Remove up to ¼" (6mm) of the wood near the edge with a 12mm (½") #3 gouge.

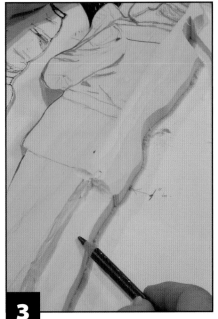

3 **Rough out the right leg.** Use a 3mm (⅛") #11 gouge to make a stop cut below the jacket. Divide the legs, using a 5mm to 7mm (³⁄₁₆" to ⁹⁄₃₂") #11 gouge or a large 90° V-tool held at a right angle to the wood surface. Remove about ¼" (6mm) from the right leg with a 20mm (¾") #9 gouge. Smooth the leg with a 12mm (½") #3 gouge.

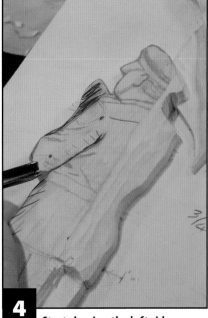

4 **Start shaping the left side.** Shade and carve the hand lower than the shoulder. Shape the back of the arm and torso with a 10mm (⅜") #11 gouge. Mark the high point of the left elbow joint with a dot and remove wood from below and to the sides of the dot to simulate taut fabric around the elbow.

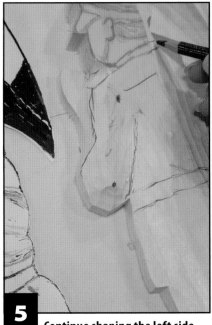

5 **Continue shaping the left side.** Use a 12mm (½") #3 gouge. Leave the wood about ½" (13mm) thick on the edge. Shape the left arm, keeping the right hand lower than the arm for proper depth and proportion. Shape the jacket from the midline of the hip down to the front edge. Redraw the collar details.

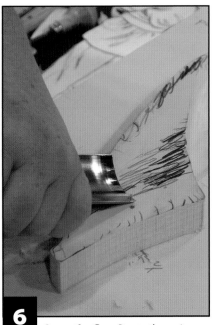

6 **Carve the flag.** Due to the grain direction, it is easier to turn the carving around to carve the deep fold in the flag. Use a 35mm (1¼") #7 gouge. Use the pattern as a guide. Round the flag edges with a 12mm (½") #3 gouge. Do not carve the top pole detail; we will add a dowel to the top in step 14.

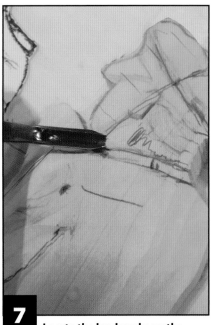

7 **Locate the landmarks on the head.** Mark the highest aspect of the hat and head with a prominent line, and do not carve on this line. The side of the left ear is the highest part of the face—treat it with care. Using a 4mm (³⁄₁₆") #11 gouge, carve behind the jaw and ear, and above the collar.

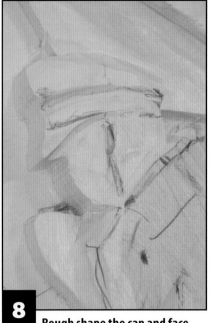

8 **Rough shape the cap and face.**
Carve under the brim of the cap. Separate the hat from the hair with a 3mm (⅛") #11 gouge. Carve from the front of the ear toward the nose with a 12mm (½") #3 gouge. Separate the chin from the shoulder. Round the hat and hair. Start behind the ear and work back.

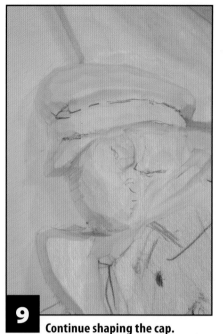

9 **Continue shaping the cap.**
Redraw the lines on the hat and mark the hairline and beard. Carve the top of the cap down toward the back where it meets the flag. The final shaping of the top of the cap will be done when the head is finalized. Carve underneath the collar with a 3mm (⅛") #11 gouge.

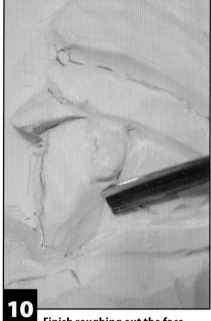

10 **Finish roughing out the face.**
Undercut the peak of the cap. Shape the right shoulder and collar area. Define the area behind the jaw and ear, using a 10mm (⅜") #9 gouge. Clean up the neck area by carving lightly toward the jaw. Now is the time to remove any rough cuts under the jaw. Draw on the face profile.

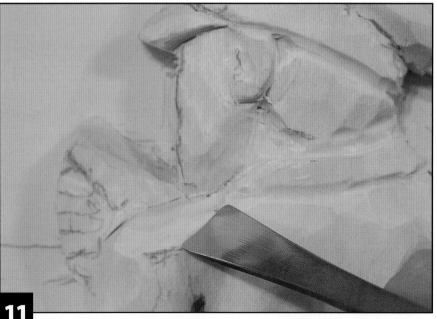

11 **Shape the left shoulder.** Finish shaping the left shoulder. Use a 12mm (½") #3 gouge; I use a fishtail. Pay particular attention to the area where the shoulder covers the hand. Much of the perspective of the carving depends on getting the angles correct in this area. Then sketch in the hand details.

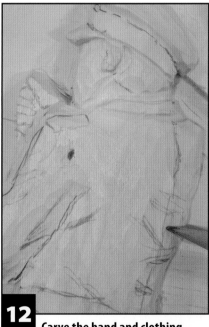

12 **Carve the hand and clothing folds.** Use a 3mm and a 5mm (⅛" and ³⁄₁₆") #11 gouge. The deeper folds are on the right and do not cross the midline of the back. Light folds cross the midline as the fabric stretches across the back. Carve the hand details with a 3mm (⅛") #11 gouge and a knife.

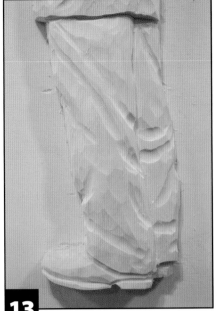

13 **Shape the legs and shoes.** Draw in the folds in the pants and shoe details, using the pattern as a guide. Then carve them with a 3mm (⅛") #11 gouge and a 7mm (¼") #11 gouge. A V-tool would make sharp creases, but the gouges create more realistic drapes and folds that resemble the folds of stiff dress pants.

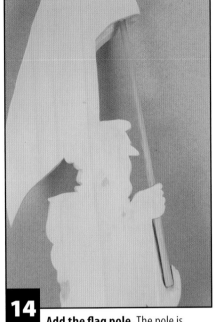

14 **Add the flag pole.** The pole is made up of three parts. Use a ruler for proper alignment. Drill holes for the dowel with a #8 drill bit. It goes into the bottom of the flag 1" (25mm) and into the top of the hand, and top of the flag ¼" (6mm). Carve a groove in the elbow and under the fingers. Cut the dowel pieces to fit.

15 **Finish shaping the face and flag.** Use caution when shaping the ear; if it looks like the side view of an ear, it's incongruent with the ¾ view of the carving. Shape and add rough texture to the beard and hair with a 3mm (⅛") #11 gouge. Finish shaping the cap. Smooth the flag with a 12mm (½") #3 gouge.

16 **Add the details.** Smooth and sand the cloth areas with 180-grit nail files and fine sandpaper. Carved fabric looks better if it has been sanded. As the figure wears gloves, do not add details to the fingers. Add the final texture to the hair and beard with a V-tool. Clean up your cuts and any fuzzy wood grain.

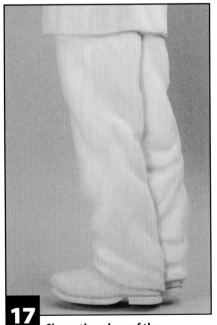

17 **Shape the edges of the carving.** Recall that we left the wood ½" (13mm) thick on the edges. Remove the carving from the plywood and carve the flat edges to flow with the folds and shape of the body and clothing. Note the left shoe is carved in side profile as his left foot is bent outward a little.

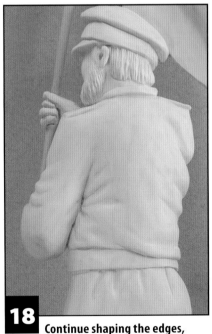

18 **Continue shaping the edges,** following the folds and shapes. This transforms the stiff, straight edges into an outline that has movement and makes the figure come alive. Glue the flag pole dowels in place.

Finishing and Painting

Saturate the finished carving with boiled linseed oil thinned with a little mineral spirits. A second coat of oil is optional but improves the sealing process. When the sealing coat is dry, spray it with a clear quick-drying lacquer. To emphasize shadows or details, apply a thin wash of burnt sienna acrylic paint mixed with water before painting the carving. Then apply your colors of choice. When dry, spray the carving with clear, quick-drying lacquer.

Caution: boiled linseed oil is flammable. Dispose of all oil-soaked rags properly.

Patterns are drawn to scale on a 1" (26mm) grid. Enlarge or reduce to desired size.

Materials & Tools

MATERIALS:

- ¾" x 5" x 20" (19mm x 130mm x 500mm) basswood
- ½"-thick plywood (larger than carving, to hold the blank while carving)
- 3 each #8 x 1" (25mm) wood screws (to secure the carving)
- ³⁄₁₆" (5mm)-diameter x 12" (300mm) dowel (flag pole)
- Nail files (180-grit or higher)
- Assorted grits of sandpaper
- Boiled linseed oil
- Mineral spirits
- Quick-dry, clear spray lacquer
- Acrylic paints of choice

TOOLS:

- Pencil, ruler, and white eraser
- Heavy duty carving support vise
- Drill and #8 bit
- Detail knife of choice
- Paint brushes
- 12mm #3 (½") gouge (fishtail optional)
- 35mm (1¼") #7 gouge (optional, can use smaller tools)
- #9 gouges: 10mm and 20mm (³⁄₈" and ¾")
- #11 gouges: 3mm, 4mm, 5mm, 7mm, and 10mm (⅛", ¹⁄₁₆", ³⁄₁₆" and ³⁄₈")
- Small V-tool
- 90° V-tool (optional)

Decorative Floral Sled

By Charley Phillips

This classic sled is a welcome change of pace from the typical Santas on holiday carving lists. It makes a beautiful decoration for your front door and can also be used as a centerpiece or displayed on your mantel.

The red-colored parts of poinsettias that most people think of as flowers are actually colored "bracts" or modified leaves. The real flowers are in the center of the colorful bracts. Poinsettias seemed a a natural embellishment for the sled, but you could adorn this project with any relief design—even a Santa if you wish!

The project is broken into different layers based on the depth of the elements. Always complete the top layer first before working on the layer below it. Paint in layers too: always base coat, shade, then highlight the elements.

Start by preparing the materials. Trace the sled and runner patterns onto the blanks with graphite paper. Cut out the sled top and runners with a reciprocating saw or band saw. You could also apply spray adhesive to the blanks and adhere a paper pattern directly to the wood. Be sure to remove the paper pattern before carving; it prevents you from seeing and working with the wood grain.

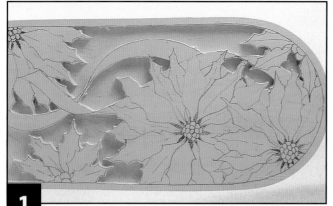

1 **Remove the background area.** Outline the inside raised border with a 30° ½" (12mm) V-tool. Outline the ribbon and leaf elements that border the background with the same tool. Do not cut more than ¼" (6mm) deep. Remove ¼" (6mm) of wood from the outlined background with a ½" (12mm) #3 gouge or a router with a spiral bit. Color code the poinsettia leaves. The top level of leaves are left natural. Color the next lower level pink, the third dark pink, and the lowest level red.

2 **Define the different levels.** Tilt a 30° ½" (12mm) V-tool away from the upper poinsettia. Make a cut perpendicular to the top surface with one edge of the tool cutting along the pattern lines, and the other edge removing wood from the lower poinsettia. Do not remove the lines on the upper poinsettia. Carve down about ⅛" (3mm), and taper it out about ½" (12mm). I use the side of the V-tool. Lower the other elements using the same technique.

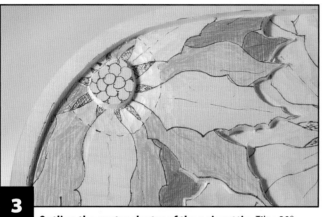

3 **Outline the center cluster of the poinsettia.** Tilt a 30° ½" (12mm) V-tool away from the flower cluster, and carve the outline of the entire flower cluster. Remove material from the leaves, carving down ⅛" (3mm). Taper down to the bottom of the V-tool cut from approximately 1" (25mm) out, with the side of the same V-tool. Redraw the pattern lines as you go.

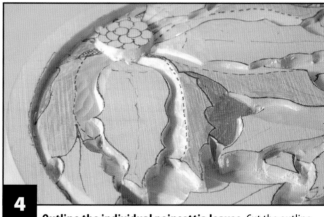

4 **Outline the individual poinsettia leaves.** Cut the outline of the natural-colored upper leaves with a 30° V-tool; use a ½" (12mm) or a ¼" (6mm) V-tool depending on the size of the work area. Carve down the side of the leaf ⅛" (3mm), and taper down to this depth from ½" (12mm) out. Redraw the pattern lines. Use the same technique to outline the light and dark pink leaves. The red leaves are not outlined.

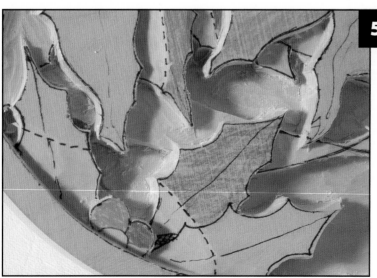

5 **Outline the holly berries.** Use a 30° ½" (12mm) V-tool to carve an outline around the cluster of holly berries. Carve into the holly leaves ⅛" (3mm), and taper down to that depth from approximately 1" (25mm) out. Use the same V-tool techniques explained above. Redraw the pattern lines. Color code the holly leaf levels as you did with the poinsettia to help establish the levels. I leave the highest leaves the natural color of the wood. The next lower level of leaves is light green, and the lowest layer of leaves is dark green.

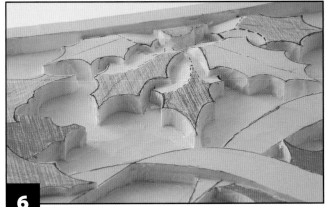

6 **Outline the holly leaves.** Use the same techniques explained in step 4. Start with the natural-colored leaves, then move on to the light green leaves. The lowest level of holly leaves, with no other elements below it, will not need to be outlined. Repeat this step for all the holly leaves. Redraw the pattern lines as you carve them away to keep the leaves symmetrical.

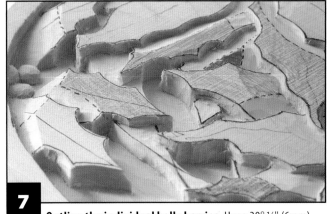

7 **Outline the individual holly berries.** Use a 30° ¼" (6mm) V-tool to outline the top berry. Then outline the next lower berry, and finally outline the lowest berry if needed. Each berry should be approximately ⅛" (3mm) lower than the one above it to make three layers of berries. Round the berries with a ⅜" (10mm) #3 gouge turned upside-down. Repeat this step on all of the holly berry clusters.

8 **Rough out the inside of the holly leaves.** Start with an uncolored leaf. Make a groove on the centerline with a ¼" (6mm) #11 veiner. It should be ⅛" (3mm) deep at the outer tip of the leaf, tapering down to ¼" (6mm) deep at the stem. Using the same tool, carve a groove from the outside edge of the leaf between each sharp point to the center groove.

9 **Blend the parts of the holly leaves together.** Hold a ⅜" (10mm) #3 gouge at a 45° angle to the centerline at the edge of the leaf. Cut toward the centerline to remove the sharp edges left by the veiner. This will create a smooth, flowing leaf. Repeat this process from the other side of the leaf. The leaf edge should have random heights along its entire length.

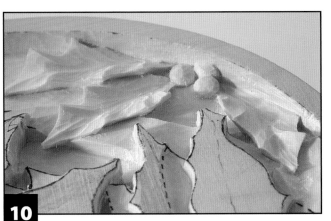

10 **Undercut the holly leaves.** Use a 30° ¼" (6mm) V-tool. The undercutting should come to a crisp edge at the outer edge of the leaf to give the illusion that the leaf is thin and sharp at all of the points. Carve all of the holly leaves, using the same techniques. Repeat steps 3 and 4 to outline each progressively lower poinsettia. Remember to work on the highest levels first. Redraw the pattern lines as you carve them away.

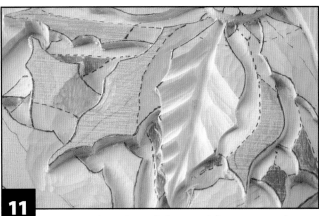

11 **Rough out the poinsettia leaves.** Make a groove on the centerline of the leaf with a ¼" (6mm) #11 veiner. The groove should be approximately ⅛" (3mm) deep at the tip of the leaf and taper down to a maximum depth of ¼" (6mm) at the stem. Cut a groove between each of the points located on the outer edge of each poinsettia leaf with the same veiner. This should run from the outside edge to the center and should be the same depth as the centerline groove.

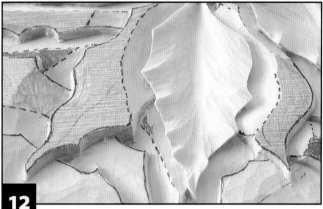

12 **Blend the leaf parts together.** Use the same tool and techniques as in step 9. Then undercut all of the poinsettia leaves with a 30° ¼" (6mm) V-tool. This should create a crisp edge at the outer edge of the leaf, giving the illusion that the leaf is thin. Use the same techniques to finish carving all of the poinsettia leaves.

13 **Round the poinsettia flower cluster.** Use a ⅜" (10mm) #3 gouge. Turn the gouge upside down to round the center. The cluster should resemble the top half of a ball. Repeat the process for all three flower clusters. Clean up the area where the leaves meet the center clusters if necessary.

14 **Carve the individual flowers.** Draw a ⅛" (3mm)-diameter circle on the center of the cluster. Hold a ⅛" (3mm) #3 gouge perpendicular to the mound, and rock the gouge side to side to score around the circle. Cut ⅛" (3mm) deep, and be careful not to undercut the flower. Round the outside edges of the first flower by holding the same gouge upside down. Repeat until all the individual flowers are carved. Carve the other flowers using the same techniques.

15 **Add the final details.** Carve the ribbon with a ½" (12mm) #3 gouge. Use a 30° ¼" (6mm) V-tool to undercut the ribbon and to create the crisp edge. Then lightly dress the background with a ⅞" (20mm) #3 gouge. Make all the chisel marks move in the same direction. Dress the back of the sled top in the same manner. Round the edges of the sled with an upside down ⅜" (10mm) #3 gouge. Lightly sand the piece to remove any remaining rough spots.

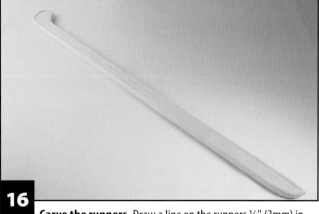

16 **Carve the runners.** Draw a line on the runners ⅛" (3mm) in from the edge. Outline inside the line with a 30° ½" (12mm) V-tool, cutting ⅛" (3mm) deep. Once outlined, relieve inside the lines with a ⅜" (10mm) #3 gouge. Round the outer edges with the same gouge turned upside down. Dress the relieved area as you did with the background on the sled.

17 **Apply a base coat to the poinsettias and the holly.** Use a 10:90 wash (10% paint to 90% retarder) of napthol red light for the poinsettia leaves and holly berries. Use a 10:90 wash of olive green and retarder for the poinsettia flower clusters and the holly leaves. Paint these with your brush of choice.

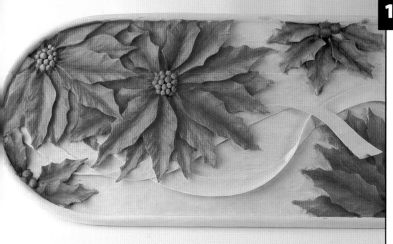

18

Apply the shading. Side load a ½" (13mm)-wide angled, flat brush with burgundy and flow medium for the poinsettia leaves. This goes on any leaf that is shadowed by an upper leaf or the poinsettia flower cluster. Blend this mixture down the center of all poinsettia leaves as well. The leaf edges should remain the shade of the original wash. Rinse the brush, and side load it with olive green and flow medium to shade the holly leaves, using the same technique. Shade the holly berries with a 75:25 mixture of burgundy and retarder, and the poinsettia flower clusters with a 75:25 mixture of olive green and retarder. Use a #6 round brush. Wipe the paint off the higher spots with a damp paper towel while the paint is still wet.

19

Highlight the poinsettias and holly. Use warm white and flow medium. Side load a ½" (13mm)-wide angled, flat brush with warm white and flow medium, and highlight the raised portions of the poinsettia and holly leaves. This transparent coating will lighten the original base coat. Use the same technique to highlight the top surface of the holly berries. Then use Naples yellow hue and a round toothpick to paint small dots on each individual poinsettia flower. Repeat to add napthol red light dots to the flowers once the yellow paint is dry.

20

Paint the rest of the sled. Use a #6 round brush to apply full-strength gold paint to the ribbon and the rounded edge of the sled. Side load a ½" (13mm)-wide angled, flat brush with burnt sienna and flow medium to shade any place where the ribbon is shadowed. Carve away any paint you splashed on the background, and sand it lightly. Apply a base coat of full-strength warm white to the background and the back side of the sled with a 1" (25mm)-wide angled, flat brush. Side load the ½" (13mm)-wide angled, flat brush with olive green and flow medium to shade the background where it is shadowed and along the gold edge. Wash the poinsettia and holly leaves with a 1:99 blend of gold and retarder, using a ½" (13mm)-wide angled, flat brush. This sheer coating will leave gold sparkles on the leaves.

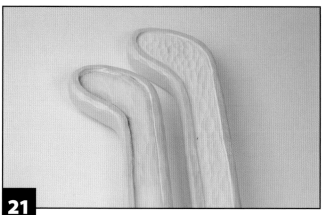

21

Paint the runners. Paint the raised edges of the runners with full-strength gold, using a ½" (13mm)-wide angled, flat brush. Paint the inside of the runners with full-strength warm white, using the same brush. Side load the same brush with olive green and flow medium to shade the inside of the runners along the raised edge. Carefully glue and clamp the runners to the sled top. Allow the paint to cure for 72 hours, then seal it with a 50:50 mixture of water-based matte varnish and water.

For definitions of painting terms, see page 85.

Photocopy at 125% or desired size

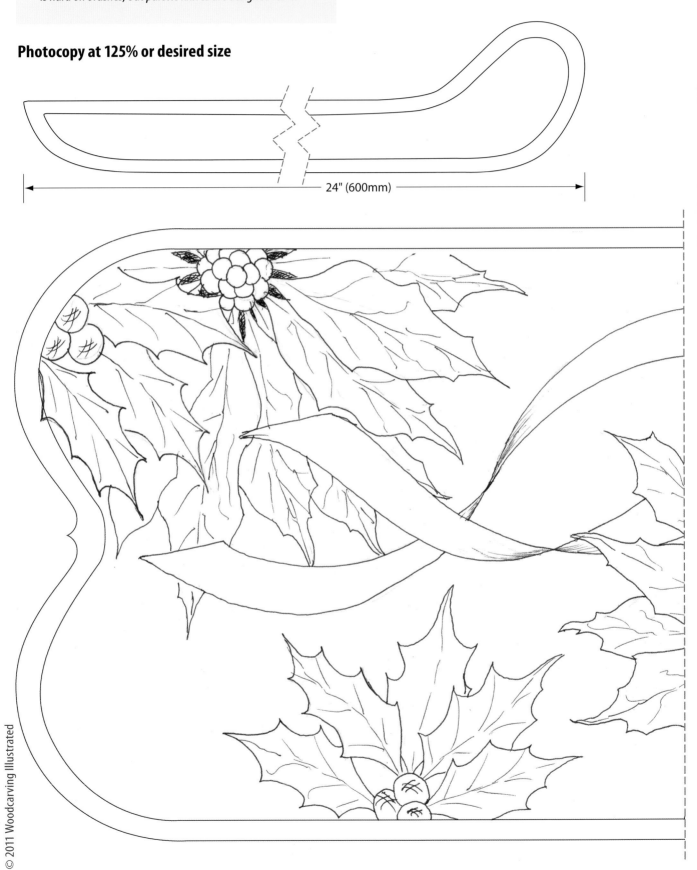

24" (600mm)

© 2011 Woodcarving Illustrated

MATERIALS:
- ½" x 8" x 18½" (12mm x 200mm x 500mm) basswood (sled)
- ½" x 3½" x 24" (12mm x 90mm x 600mm) basswood (runners)
- Two copies of the pattern
- Spray adhesive
- Wood glue
- Graphite paper

FINISHING MATERIALS:
- 1-quart water container (to rinse brushes in)
- Disposable palette paper
- Bubble palette
- Water-based matte varnish
- Gel retarder or retarder medium
- Flow medium
- Brushes: ½" (13mm)-wide angled, flat; 1" (25mm)-wide angled, flat; #6 round
- Acrylic paints:
  Napthol red light
  Olive green
  Burgundy
  Naples yellow hue
  Warm white
  Gold
  Burnt sienna

- Palette knife
- Round toothpicks

TOOLS:
- #3 gouges: ⅛", ⅜", ½", and ⅞" (3mm, 10mm, 12mm, and 20mm)
- ¼" (6mm) #11 veiner
- 30° ½" (12mm) V-tool
- 30° ¼" (6mm) V-tool
- Carving knife of choice
- Reciprocating saw or band saw

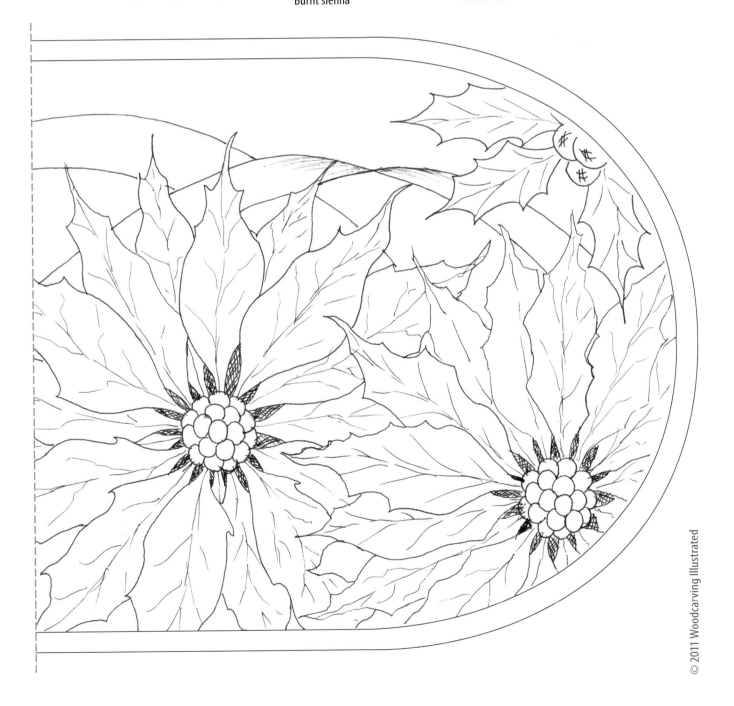

© 2011 Woodcarving Illustrated

Relief Carved Sunflower Clock

By Charley Phillips

Sunflowers are a classic symbol of summer and look great with any decor. The design is perfect for an elegant clock, or you can use the flowers to embellish a variety of projects.

Start by preparing your blank. Cut your wood into a 12" (300mm) circle. Locate the center on the back and mark it. With a 3" (76mm)-diameter Forstner bit, drill ⅝" (16mm) into the wood at the center mark. Next drill a ⁵⁄₁₆" (8mm)-diameter hole completely through the wood in the center. The shaft of the clock movement will need to fit through the ⁵⁄₁₆" (8mm)-diameter hole; the clock movement will fit in the 3" (75mm)-diameter recess in the back of the clock. Glue the pattern to the front of the clock.

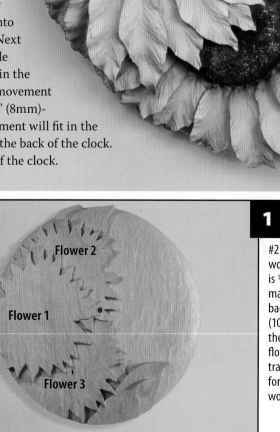

Flower 2

Flower 1

Flower 3

1

Block in the various levels. Remove the wood for flower #2 so the entire surface is ¹/₈" (3mm) below the surface of the wood. Remove the wood for flower #3 and leaf #3 so the surface is ¹/₈" (3mm) below the surface of flower #2. Repeat this process, making each number ¹/₈" (3mm) lower than the previous and the background ¹/₈" (3mm) lower than the lowest flower. Use a #2³/₈" (10mm) gouge; use a router to speed the process if you wish. From the pattern, trace flower #2 and #3 onto tracing paper. Cut each flower from the tracing paper. Position graphite paper under the tracing paper and trace the flowers onto the wood. If the pattern for flower #1 is damaged, remove the remaining pattern from the wood, and trace this flower also.

2 **Cut an outline of the center of flower #1.** Tilt a 30° ½"
(12mm) V-tool away from the circle you are outlining to create
a cut perpendicular to the top surface of the circle. This outline
should be approximately 5/16" (8mm) deep and should blend back
into the surface of the wood approximately ¾" (19mm) from the
edge of the circle. Repeat the process on flowers #2 and #3.

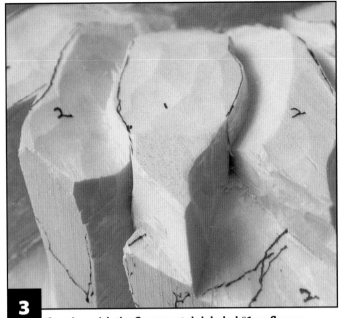

3 **Starting with the flower petals labeled #1 on flower
#1, outline each flower petal with a 30° ½" (12mm) V-tool.**
Follow the technique used in Step 1. This outline should be ⅛"
(3mm) deep. Complete this process for all #1 flower petals. On the
flower petals adjacent to petal #1, blend from the outline toward the
opposite edge of the flower petal, using a #3 ¼" (6mm) gouge.

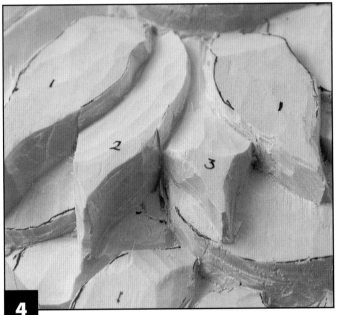

4 **Repeat this process to all the flower petals bordering
the #1 petals.** Using a 30° ½" (12mm) V-tool, repeat the
outlining process for all the exposed edges of flower petals #2.
Blend all the flower petals adjacent to the #2 petals, using a #3
¼" (6mm) gouge. Blend from the groove created by the outline
of the flower petal toward the square edge of the opposite side of
the petal. This should make all #3 flower petals ⅛" (2mm) below
adjacent flower petals. Using a #3 ¼" (6mm) gouge, carve the
outer third of each flower petal down 1/16" to ¼" (2mm to 6mm) to
random levels, creating an arc.

5 **Make a groove on the centerline of the #1 petals with
a #11 ¼" (6mm) veiner.** The groove should be ⅛" (2mm) deep
at the outer tip, getting progressively deeper toward the center
of the flower, to a maximum depth of ¼" (6mm). Blend the petal
by starting at the tip and working toward the center of the flower.
Using the same tool at a 30° angle to the centerline, work from
one edge toward the centerline, removing more wood as you
move toward the center. Repeat this process from the other side of
the petal. Separate the petals as you approach the center as well.
Random heights along the petal's edge give a natural wavy look.

6 **Undercut all #1 petals.** Use a 24° ¼" (6mm) V-tool, or the narrowest V-tool available. Complete all #1 petals and repeat steps 5 and 6 on all #2 petals, then #3 petals. Repeat steps 3 through 6 on flower #2 and then flower #3. Detail the area where the petals meet the center of the flower with a carving knife.

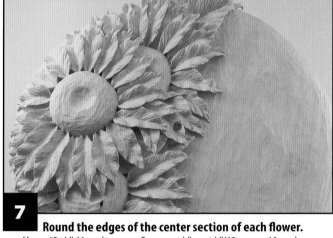

7 **Round the edges of the center section of each flower.** Use a #3 ¼" (6mm) gouge. Create a ½"- to ¾"(13mm to 19mm)-diameter depression ⅛" (3mm) deep in the center of each flower using the same tool. This adds to the realistic look of the carving.

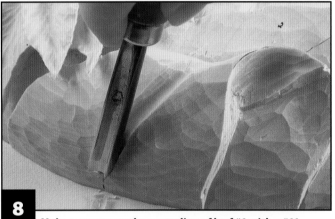

8 **Make a groove on the centerline of leaf #1 with a #11 ¼" (6mm) veiner.** The process to make the leaves is identical to the process of making each flower petal. The groove should be ⅛" (2mm) deep at the outer tip of the leaf, getting progressively deeper toward the stem of the leaf, to a maximum depth of ½" (13mm).

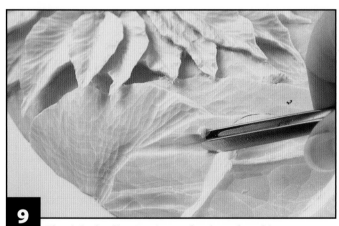

9 **Blend the leaf by starting at the tip and working toward the stem.** Hold the veiner at a 30° angle to the centerline, and work from one of the edges toward the centerline, removing more wood as you move toward the center. Vary the depth and height of the edges to achieve a natural wavy look.

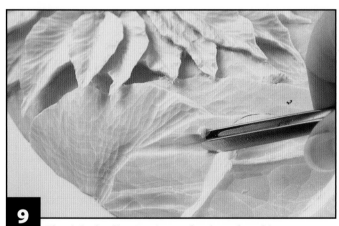

10 **Undercut the leaf with a 24° ¼" (6mm) V-tool, or the narrowest V-tool available.** Repeat the process to all of the leaves in consecutive order. Always complete any leaf on top of another, before starting a lower leaf. Using a #3⅞" (25mm) gouge, round the outside edge of background. Use a small piece of sandpaper folded in half to clean up any fuzzies.

Materials & Tools

MATERIALS:
- 1¼" x 12" x 12" (32mm x 305mm x 305mm) basswood
- Aerosol spray adhesive
- 2 copies of the pattern
- Graphite paper
- Tracing paper
- Clock movement & hands

FINISHING MATERIALS:
- Retarder
- Water-based varnish
- Palette knife
- Disposable palette paper

- Bubble palette
- Water container
- Brushes:
  ½" (13mm) angled flat
  ¾" (19mm) angled flat
  ½" (13mm) flat
  1" (25mm) flat
  #6 round
  ¼" (6mm) deerfoot
- Acrylic paint:
  Naples yellow hue
  Indian yellow
  Diox purple
  Burnt sienna
  Burnt umber
  French blue

Napthol red light
Raw sienna
Titanium white
Black

TOOLS:
- #2 ⅜" (10mm) gouge
- #3 gouges: ¼" and ⅞" (6mm and 20mm)
- #11 ¼" (6mm) veiner
- 24° ¼" (6mm) V-tool
- 30° ½" (12mm) V-tool
- Carving knife of choice

PAINTING THE SUNFLOWER CLOCK

...finitions of several specific painting terms I use ...e listed below. When painting, always basecoat, ...en shade, then highlight. When mixing, always ...e a palette knife, not a brush. If you mix with a ...ush, it could damage the brush.

PAINTING TERMS

Basecoating: Painting an entire object or specific area with paint at full strength or using a wash of paint.

Wash: A 10:90 mixture of paint and retarder blended in a bubble palette. When applied to a wood surface, a wash will create a slight tint of color so the wood grain can show through.

Side Load/Float: A technique used to apply shading or highlights. Dip the brush in water, and then lightly blot the brush on a paper towel to remove the excess water. Dip one corner of the brush into the paint, and palette blend back and forth several times to blend the paint into the brush. Take care that the color does not float to the opposite corner of the brush. One side of the brush must remain clear. If color has bled over to the other side, rinse the brush, and start over.

Double Side Load/Double Dip: After side loading the brush with one color and palette blending, dip the corner of the brush holding the paint into a second color. Palette-blend the brush again.

Dry Brushing: A technique used to lighten or darken a surface. Using a dry brush, pick up a small amount of paint. Then work the brush back and forth on the palette until almost free of paint. Apply with light strokes across the surface.

Stippling: A technique to create a fuzzy-looking texture to a surface. Using a dry deerfoot brush, dip the brush lightly into paint, and bounce it up and down on your palette to remove all the excess paint. Apply the paint by bouncing up and down on the desired surface. Apply the paint lightly to allow some of the basecoat to show through; this will leave a fuzzy appearance.

1 **Create a 90:10 mixture of Naples yellow hue and Indian yellow paint.** Add a spot of diox purple the size of a pen dot. Basecoat all the petals with a wash of this mixture using the 3/4" (19mm) angled flat brush. Do not basecoat the background. If you get paint on the background, carve it off the wood.

3 **Shade all the flower petals that are below any adjoining petals.** Create a 90:10 mixture of Naples yellow hue and Indian yellow. Using a 1/2" (13mm) angled flat brush, side load the brush with the yellow mixture, then dip the side-loaded brush into raw sienna, and blend this into the brush.

5 **Side load the brush with Naples yellow hue paint and highlight the raised areas of each petal.** Also, highlight all the petal tips not darkened in step 4. Then highlight approximately a third to a half of all the petal's raised areas with titanium white.

2 **Basecoat the center of the flower with a wash of burnt sienna.** Blend a fifty-cent-sized 50:50 mix of French blue and Indian yellow, and put 25% of it in an airtight container to use later. Basecoat the leaves with a wash of the mixture.

4 **Shade all the petals where the petals attach in the center of the flower.** Create a 99:1 mixture of raw sienna and just a pen dot of napthol red light paint and shade the areas using the side load technique. Randomly shade approximately a quarter to a third of the petal tips.

6 **Stipple a mixture of burnt umber and a dab of retarder on the center of each flower.** Use a deerfoot brush. This process should be light enough to allow some of the background color to show through.

7 **Stipple a mixture of raw sienna plus a dab of retarder on the center of each flower.** Use a deerfoot brush. This process should be light enough to allow some of the background color and the burnt umber to show through.

8 **Very lightly stipple a mixture of Naples yellow hue and a dab of retarder on the center of the flower.** Use a deerfoot brush. Keep this process light enough to allow most of the background colors to show through.

9 **Shade the center vein and area of each leaf that is under another leaf or below a flower.** Using the mix blended in step 2, add a pen dot of black paint and mix. Side load a ¹⁄₂" (13mm) angled flat brush with this mixture for the shading.

10 **Side load a ¹⁄₂" (13mm) angled flat brush with Naples yellow hue.** Highlight the raised areas and tips of the leaves and allow them to dry. Use the same brush and color to dry brush the leaves, highlighting the chisel marks.

11 **Side load a ¹⁄₂" (13mm) angled flat brush with burnt sienna.** Make a few random-sized, uneven, circular brown spots on the leaves for a realistic look. Carve off any paint you may have inadvertently splashed on the background.

12 **Paint the background with a 1" (25mm) flat brush** and a 75:25 mixture of Naples yellow hue and titanium white. After drying, basecoat the area where the blue flowers will be with a light wash of retarder using a ¹⁄₂" (13mm) flat brush.

13 **Paint translucent flowers with a #6 round brush.** Use a mixture of 50:50 French blue and titanium white with a light wash of retarder. Add white to the mixture as you near the tips.

14 **Shade the background** under the sunflowers and leaves, including the area over the blue flowers. Use a side loaded ³⁄₄" (19mm) angled flat brush loaded with burnt sienna.

15 **Allow the paint to cure for 72 hours.** Seal it with a 50:50 mixture of water and water-based varnish to produce a matte finish. Complete the project by installing the clock components.

Drawing resides on a 1"
(25mm) grid to the scale
of the original carving.
Photocopy at 144%
or desired size

Flower 2

Flower 1

Flower 3

© 2011 Woodcarving Illustrated

Creating a Deep-Relief Mantel

By Jerry Mifflin

A hand-carved mantel adds instant value to your home. Approaching the mantel as individual panels with a repeating design breaks it down into chunks and makes it more manageable. The traditional oak leaf design can also be used to embellish a variety of other projects, such as a mirror frame, door topper, or hope chest. For a simpler version, see page 92.

I use actual leaves from my backyard to create the pattern and then separate the pattern into five separate levels or layers based on the depth of the cuts. Each layer is separated by ⅛" (3mm) to ¼" (6mm). Shade the leaves in the different layers to assist you as you rough them out. Work from the lowest level of the carving to the highest level in each stage. Do not carve the acorns until all the layers of leaves have been finished.

The wood must be secured to a workbench, especially during the stop-cut process, as both hands are needed to control the router. Use scrap strips of wood against bench dogs to protect the edges of the panel.

To keep the carving surface clear and to make cleaning up easy, hold the nozzle of a shop vacuum in your off hand when carving with a flexible-shaft tool. I'm right-handed, so I hold the nozzle in my left hand. Position the nozzle 2" to 4" (50mm to 100mm) away from the carving. You can mount the nozzle close to where you are carving, but holding the nozzle helps collect the dust at the source and keeps the dust from obscuring the area where you are working.

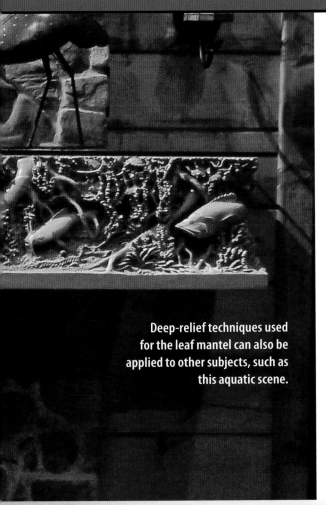

Deep-relief techniques used for the leaf mantel can also be applied to other subjects, such as this aquatic scene.

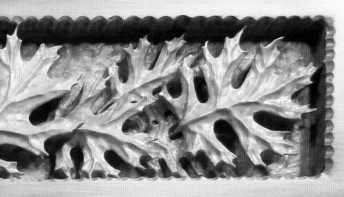

Hold the handpiece of the rotary power carver like a pencil, with the heel of your hand and your forearm resting on the wood surface for stability. To control the cut path, hold the handpiece at a 45° angle, leaning in the direction of the cut. Move the burr in the direction of the rotation to avoid digging into the wood.

Transfer the design to the blank by taping the pattern to the wood using removable painter's tape. Slip graphite transfer paper under the pattern and trace the pattern onto the blank. Trace the lines on the blank with a marker for better visibility.

The lettered boxes inset into the step photos indicate the bits used, referring to the chart on page 90.

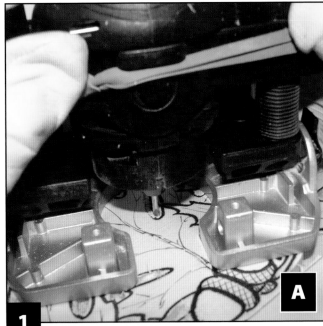

1 **Outline the elements.** Use a rotary power carver with a router attachment and bit A. Stay ¹⁄₁₆" (2mm) away from the pattern lines as you stop-cut ¼" (6mm) deep around the elements. Remove the waste between the stop cuts. Continue making passes, increasing the depth of cut by ¼" (6mm) each time, until the background depth is 1" (25mm).

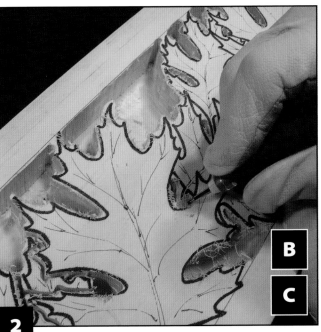

2 **Separate the leaves.** Use a flexible-shaft tool and bit B. Make stop cuts perpendicular to the outline of each leaf, keeping ¹⁄₁₆" (2mm) away from the line. Make several passes until the stop cuts are ¼" (6mm) deep. Make the stop cuts deeper and wider with bit C. The stop cuts are deeper at the stem than at the tip.

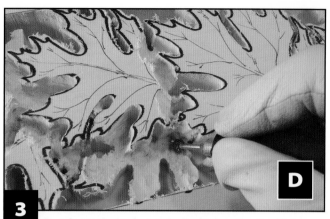

3

Rough out the lower levels. Use bit D and begin with the lowest layer, reducing the leaves to approximately ¹⁄₁₆" (2mm) above the background at their stems. For each leaf, the stem is about ¼" (6mm) lower than the tip. Work up through consecutive layers to layer 3. Each of the five layers is ⅛" (3mm) to ¼" (6mm) higher than the one below it.

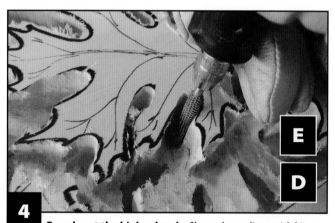

4

Rough out the higher levels. Shape the outlines with bit E. Use bit D to reduce the leaves in layers 1 and 2, maintaining ⅛" (3mm) difference in the depth between layers. Use the same bit to deepen the background ¼" (6mm) at all of the stems and to overlap sections of leaves. Avoid the acorns.

Bit Indentification Chart

BIT	SIZE	SHAPE	TYPE
A	⅛" (3.1mm)	safe-end cylinder	carbide bit
B	¹⁄₁₆" (1.6mm)	cylinder	carbide bit
C	³⁄₃₂" (2.3mm)	ball-nose	carbide bit
D	⁵⁄₁₆" (8mm)	ball	extra-coarse carbide-point bit
E	³⁄₁₆" (5mm)	ball-nose cylinder	coarse carbide-point bit
F	⁷⁄₁₆" (10mm)	ball	coarse carbide-point bit
G	⁷⁄₁₆" (10mm)	ball	fine carbide-point bit
H	³⁄₁₆" (5mm)	tapered	extra-coarse carbide-point bit
I	¼" (6mm)	ball	ruby bit
J	⅛" (3.1mm)	tapered	coarse ruby bit
K	⅛" (3mm)	ball	carbide bit
L	³⁄₁₆" (5mm)	ball	carbide bit
M	⁵⁄₁₆" (8mm)	ball	fine carbide-point bit
N	⅜" (10mm)	ball	blue ceramic stone
O	³⁄₁₆" (5mm)	ball	green ceramic stone
P	³⁄₃₂" (2.5mm)	ball	fine diamond bit
Q	¼" (6.2mm)	ball-nose cylinder	white ceramic stone
R	³⁄₁₆" (5mm)	ball	white ceramic stone
S	¼" (6mm)	tapered	white ceramic stone

5

Rough shape the leaves. Use bit F. Leave a ridge down the main and secondary veins of the leaves. Create a valley in the curved areas between lobes, tapering out to the edges of the lobes. Scoop out some of the lobes so the tips curl up and shape others to turn down at the tip. Use the photo as a guide.

6

Carve the border. Draw a line ¼" (6mm) outside the border. Hold a ⅝" (16mm) #5 gouge at a 45° angle and carve from the new line toward the open space around the leaves. Hold the same gouge vertically, in line with the initial cut, and cut straight down, stopping just before the background. Release the chip from the leaf side.

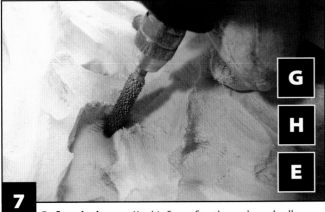

7 **Refine the leaves.** Use bit G to refine the peaks and valleys of the leaves. Shape, but do not undercut, the edges with bit H. Use bit E to carve the background around the stems and the lobes down to 1¼" (30mm), tapering it up to 1" (25mm) deep at the lobe tips.

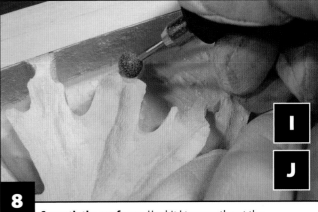

8 **Smooth the surfaces.** Use bit I to smooth out the background around the leaves and at the bottom of the border. Use this same bit to smooth the leaves and add more definition to the veins and curling of the lobe tips. Use bit J to further define the stems, leaving them thicker than normal at this stage.

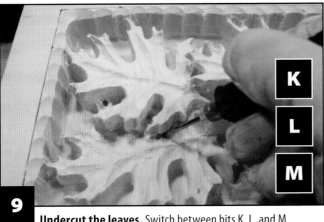

9 **Undercut the leaves.** Switch between bits K, L, and M depending on the distance between the surface of the leaf and the background. Taper the cut downward toward the center of the lobe or leaf body. Leave the edges of the leaves ¹⁄₁₆" to ³⁄₃₂" (2mm to 3mm) thick.

10 **Refine the undercuts.** Deepen the undercut to the background on some leaves. Use the photo as a guide. To keep the leaves from becoming too fragile, leave some tips attached to other leaves or the border for strength. Maintain a background depth of about 1³⁄₈" (35mm), tapering up to 1" (25mm) deep along the border.

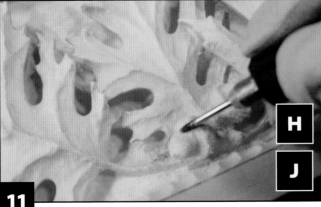

11 **Carve the acorns.** Rough out the acorns with bit H. Make ⅛" (3mm)-deep stop cuts to separate the nuts from the caps. Sketch in centerlines and round the acorns on both sides of that line. Carve the nuts ⅛" (3mm) smaller in diameter than the caps. Make both acorns the same size. Smooth the acorns with bit J.

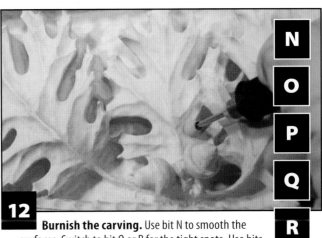

12 **Burnish the carving.** Use bit N to smooth the surfaces. Switch to bit O or P for the tight spots. Use bits Q, R, and S for a polished finish.

Oak leaf mantel pattern

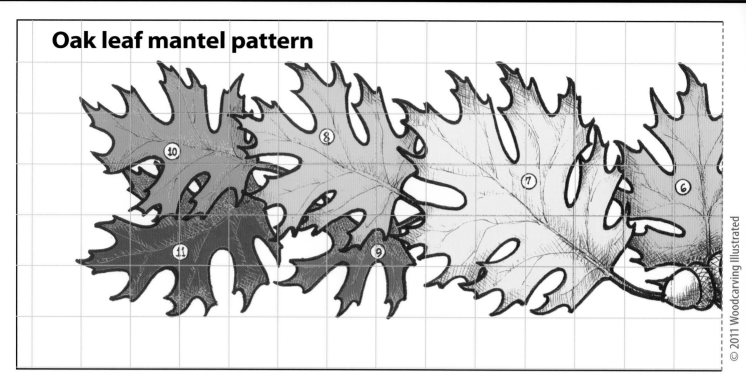

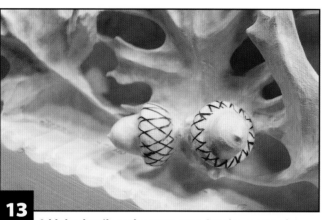

13 **Add the details to the acorn caps.** Pencil in a series of *V*s at a 45° angle along the edge of the cap. Extend each right leg up toward the stem, stopping ⅛" (3mm) short of the stem. Repeat the process for the left legs to create a diamond pattern. Burn along the lines with a woodburner on a medium to low setting, using a ⅛" (3mm)-wide skew tip. Clean the lines with an abrasive pad.

Finishing

Use 80- and then 100-grit sandpaper on the uncarved surface of the border to provide a smooth finish and allow good absorption of the stain. Remove the sanding dust and coat the entire piece with pre-stain wood conditioner. Use a soft-bristle paintbrush to apply a liberal amount of stain/sealer to the entire piece, including the back and undersides of the leaves. Blot your staining brush on a rag and use the dry brush to pick up any excess stain. Let the stain dry thoroughly, then run your fingers over the surface, feeling for any rough spots. Lightly sand any rough spots with 400-grit sandpaper and remove any sanding dust.

Use satin-finish spray lacquer for a final finish coat. Get close to the surface and spray from various angles. When dry, sand any rough surfaces with 400-grit sandpaper. Remove any dust and apply a second coat.

A Simpler Version

Don't be intimidated by large, seemingly complex projects. Approaching them one step at a time makes them much more manageable. However, if you find deep-relief carving a bit daunting, you can easily translate the pattern into a shallow or low relief by reducing the depth of the background, the separation between the different elements, and the undercutting. The low-relief version uses the same tools and techniques used in the deep-relief project, but its background is ⅞" (22mm) at deepest, with most at ¾" (19mm). The deepest part of the large center leaf is ⅜" (60mm). Instead of undercutting the elements as demonstrated in the main project, remove only ¼" (6mm) of wood from the edges of the perimeter of the leaves. The stems require only a hint of an undercut.

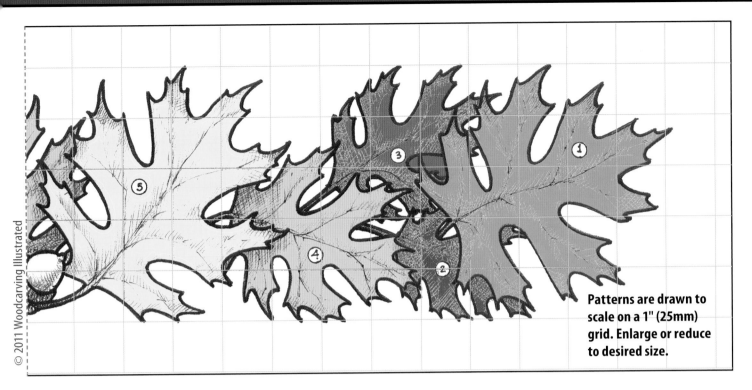

Patterns are drawn to scale on a 1" (25mm) grid. Enlarge or reduce to desired size.

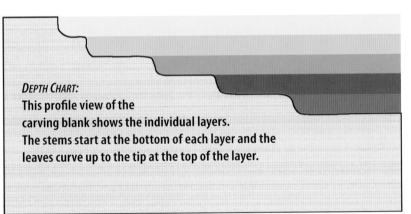

DEPTH CHART:
This profile view of the carving blank shows the individual layers. The stems start at the bottom of each layer and the leaves curve up to the tip at the top of the layer.

Layer 1: (Closest to surface) Leaves #5 and #7

Layer 2: Leaves #4, #6, and #8

Layer 3: Leaves #1 and #10

Layer 4: Leaves #2 and #11

Layer 5: (Closest to background) Leaves #3 and #9

MATERIALS:
- 2" x 7" x 28¾" (51mm x 178mm x 730mm) basswood or wood of choice (2 or more panels needed for full-size mantel)
- Graphite transfer paper
- Pre-stain wood conditioner
- Stain/sealer of choice
- Satin-finish spray lacquer
- Sandpaper: 80, 100, and 400 grits

TOOLS:
- Rotary cutting tool with ⅛" (3mm)-diameter collet
- Router attachment
- Flexible shaft attachment with ⅛" (3mm)- and ³⁄₃₂" (4mm)-diameter collets
- ⅝" (16mm) #5 gouge, or reciprocating carver with ⅝" (16mm) #5 gouge attachment
- Wood burner with ⅛"-wide skew tip

- Medium and small soft-bristle brushes for applying stain/sealer
- Abrasive pad (to clean up woodburning)

BITS:
(A) ⅛" (3.1mm)-diameter safe-end cylinder-shaped carbide bit

(B) ¹⁄₁₆" (1.6mm)-diameter cylinder-shaped carbide bit

(C) ³⁄₃₂" (2.3mm)-diameter ball-nose carbide bit

(D) ⁵⁄₁₆" (8mm)-diameter ball-shaped extreme carbide-point tip

(E) ³⁄₁₆" (5mm) -diameter ball-nose cylinder-shaped coarse carbide-point bit

(F) ⁷⁄₁₆" (10mm)-diameter ball-shaped coarse carbide-point bit

(G) ⁷⁄₁₆" (10mm)-diameter ball-shaped fine carbide-point bit

(H) ³⁄₁₆" (5mm)-diameter tapered extreme carbide-point bit

(I) ¼" (6mm)-diameter ball-shaped ruby bit

(J) ⅛" (3.1mm)-diameter tapered coarse ruby bit

(K) ⅛" (3mm)-diameter ball-shaped carbide bit

(L) ³⁄₁₆" (5mm)-diameter ball-shaped carbide bit

(M) ⁵⁄₁₆" (8mm)-diameter ball-shaped fine carbide-point bit

(N) ⅜" (10mm)-diameter blue ceramic ball-shaped stone

(O) ³⁄₁₆" (5mm)-diameter green ceramic ball-shaped stone

(P) ³⁄₃₂" (2.5mm)-diameter ball-shaped fine diamond bit

(Q) ¼" (6.2mm)-diameter white ceramic ball-nose cylinder-shaped stone

(R) ³⁄₁₆" (5mm)-diameter white ceramic ball-shaped stone

(S) ¼" (6mm)-diameter white ceramic tapered stone

Lettering, Signs, and Cards

Incorporating words and numbers adds a whole new avenue of uses for your relief carving skills. Alphabet blocks, signs, and award plaques are natural choices, and the authors in this chapter stress that once you know the techniques, you can use them to make any number of personalized projects. These projects go beyond basic carving, teaching you two different gilding techniques and how to paint signs for outdoor use. Finally, the holiday card project shows you how a basic block printing procedure can turn a single carving into a cheery handmade greeting for everyone you know.

House Sign,
by Francis S. Lestingi,
page 104

Heirloom Alphabet Blocks

By Frederick Wilbur

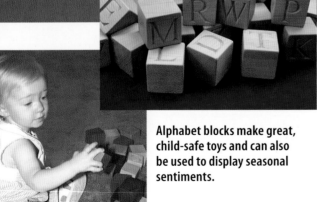

Alphabet blocks make great, child-safe toys and can also be used to display seasonal sentiments.

A welcome gift that can be passed down through generations, alpha blocks make a great holiday decoration when arranged to display classic messages.

Lettering provides a chance to develop great detail skills. Traditic Roman-style letters in the upper case are best to start with, as they the basis from which other styles are derived and fit nicely on a squ plane. The advantage of carving blocks is that if you are unhappy w one letter, you can discard the block and start over—you have not carved an entire sign.

Use durable woods such as mahogany, cherry, walnut, poplar, or s maple. The best block size is 2" (50mm) square—large enough not t be a choking hazard, but small enough for little ones to pick up easi

1 **Cut a long piece of stock to 2⅛" x 2⅛" (55mm x 55mm).** Run it through a planer or smooth it with a belt sander until it is exactly 2" x 2" (50mm x 50mm). Cut off 2" (50mm) sections. Sand the end grain smooth—you do not want to carve the letters in the end grain.

2 **Mark the faces on the cubes.** Create a ⅛" (3mm) border, marking the top line, base line, and sides. I use a pencil gauge (shown above), but a pencil and square will also work. This border defines the boundaries of most letters.

3 **Clamp the blocks for safe carving.** Fix parallel fences on a piece of plywood that fit tightly on two sides of the blocks. Place several blocks between these fences; add smaller fences to the ends so the blocks don't slide sideways. Secure the blocks with wooden wedges. You can also clamp individual blocks in a vise.

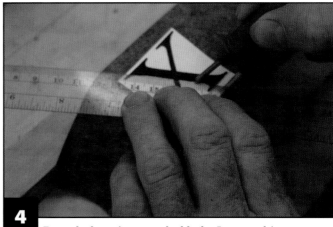

4 **Trace the lettering onto the blocks.** For most of the letters, I used 135-point Times New Roman font. Most word processing programs allow you to change the size of your font. You can also photocopy the letter patterns included here. Place graphite paper under the letters and trace them onto the blocks. A straightedge may help you get crisp lines on straight letters.

5 **Incise the main lines on the straight letters.** All carved letters rely on shadow for readability. The serif helps demarcate the end of the letter. The valleys of the narrower sections of the letters (the curve at the bottom of the *J*, for example) are not as deep as the broader ones. Use a #1 straight chisel to make a stop cut down the center of the straight letters. Using the same chisel, cut at a 50° angle to clean out the letters and make them deep.

6 **Carve in the serifs.** The serifs are the "tags" at the end of the straight lines in Roman letters. Use a modified, straight-fishtail chisel with a bevel on only one side to cut the triangular-shaped serifs. I use just the wing of the fishtail chisel to make the initial triangle.

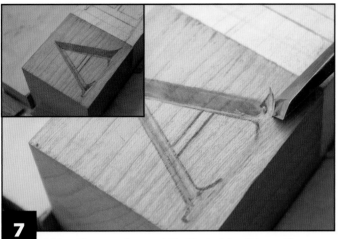

7 **Add a chip-carved pyramid to the inside of the serifs.** Incline the base of the chisel to remove the chip cleanly. Work from the extreme angles of the pyramid and shave in a curve between the serif and the body of the letter.

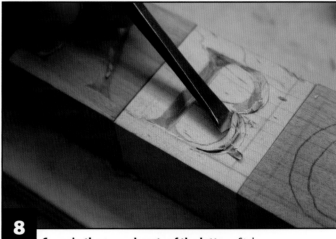

8 **Carve in the curved parts of the letters.** Stab an appropriate-sized gouge into the center of the curve to make a stop cut. Then angle in from the outside of the curve to clean out the letter. Turn the gouge over and angle in from the inside of the curve to make the valley. If this doesn't work, use the fishtail chisel to shear around the inside of the curve.

9 **Erase the layout lines.** These lines interfere with the visual clarity of the letter. If you need to sharpen up a letter, use the fishtail chisel. It is possible to use a V-tool to clean up the deep valleys, but these tools will not create crisp intersections such as the top of a *T*.

10 **Sand the block.** Use 220-grit sandpaper to smooth all the faces and round over the corners. Do not sand the valleys of the letters. Apply your finish of choice.

CHOOSING THE RIGHT GOUGE   **TIP**

The #5 gouge works well for the smaller curves, such as P and R. A #7 gouge works well for the round part at the bottom of a J. A #3 gouge will work for the rest of the curved letters.

Materials & Tools

MATERIALS:
- 2" x 2" x 2" (50mm x 50mm x 50mm) hardwood blocks (for each letter)
- Graphite paper
- Sandpaper, 220 grit
- Finish of choice (see "Child-safe finishes" below)

TOOLS:
- Block clamp or vise
- Square

- Pencil gauge (optional)
- ⅝" (16mm) #1 straight chisel
- ⅜" (10mm) modified fishtail chisel with a bevel on only one side
- ⁵⁄₁₆" (8mm) #3 gouge
- ⁵⁄₁₆" (8mm) #5 gouge
- ⁵⁄₁₆" (8mm) #7 gouge
- V-tool of choice
- Pencil

Child-safe finishes

At 2" square, these blocks are really too large for children to put in their mouths and chew on—but it is still something to think about. You could choose not to finish the blocks at all, but when the blocks get dirty, they are not as attractive. Another option is to apply an oil finish following the manufacturers' directions exactly. For example, one brand of Danish oil takes 21 days to cure completely, according to the label. So if you choose an oil finish, allow time for it to dry completely. Another alternative is a food-safe finish such as walnut oil.

ABCDEFGHIJKLMNOPQRSTUVWXYZ

Carve a Sign

By Andy Fairchok

Photography by Roger Schroeder

Commanding attention and suggesting permanence, hand-carved signs have many applications. I particularly enjoy seeing them announce a house number or family name.

For my sign, I chose a parchment scroll design with all four edges curled forward.

Before starting, you need to understand the curls. To visualize how they should look, make concave cuts on both ends of a piece of paper. Roll the paper from the top or bottom, and the curls will appear.

Because wood does not bend easily, I form the appearance of "rolls" by adding narrow strips of wood to the sign, then make the "curls" by carving the ends.

Perfect Pine

When selecting wood for your sign, remember that many woods are easy to carve, but some do not hold up outdoors. Basswood, for instance, rots quickly once the protective finish wears away. On the other hand, cedar and redwood withstand the elements, but they are not easy to carve.

I recommend eastern white pine because it carves crisply and accepts most finishes. When sealed properly, it stands up to the weather. Where I live, the species is fairly common and relatively inexpensive. Consider using boards with knots; they are often cheaper, and the wood between the knots is as good as the clear variety.

The ABCs of Sign Carving

The array of lettering styles available is almost staggering. Alphabets and numbers range from simple block forms to creations ornate enough to make even a Victorian wince. Many can be taken from word processing programs, but I find that styles with some fluidity are much more appealing than fonts such as Arial, which are often used on computers.

My sign combines two slanting script styles. The one I will demonstrate in the instructions uses the word *fox*, which has essential curves and straight lines that will apply to any name or number combination you choose.

Essential Tools

After carving the ends of the curls with two or three different gouges, I start shaping the letters with a V-tool. This removes waste wood and establishes the trough of each incised letter, a look that is very appealing on a carved sign.

V-tool angles range from 24° to more than 90°; which you choose depends on the width and depth of the incision you desire. For example, a narrow V-tool makes deep letters and numbers. A 60° V-tool works well for this project.

Chisels and gouges are also essential, with sizes depending on the shapes of the lettering. Long curves require fairly flat gouges. I prefer a #3 gouge whenever possible because it does not create unsightly steps when cleaning up the walls of the incisions, instead leaving facets that are much easier to pare away later.

I recommend fishtail gouges instead of straight ones; it is easier to see what the cutting edge is doing, and they clean up the corners in serifs more easily.

A carving knife is also useful, particularly when working with serifs; the sharp point gets into tight corners that defy even the smallest gouge or chisel.

Finishing Touches

After finishing the carving, lightly remove the surface pencil marks with a sponge sander, being careful not to touch the insides of the letters. Even where slight facets or gouge marks are unavoidable, sanding gives a machine-carved look. Tool marks make it clear to the viewer that the project was done by hand.

Before applying the finish, take the sign outdoors and look carefully at the carved lettering. A different light source quickly reveals places that need more work. I often wait a day before I take a close second look at the sign.

If the trough of an incised letter is poorly defined, the apex of your V-tool may be too flat. You can correct the problem with a double-beveled straight chisel, tapping it lightly with a mallet as you follow the trough of the letter. This better defines and sharpens the letters. An alternative is to use a burning pen with a sharp tip at a moderate heat setting.

After cleaning off the sanding dust, seal the sign with two or three coats of shellac for a nice mellow tone. Seal knots if they are present. A very light sanding and a spray coat of polyurethane also produce a fairly weather-resistant finish.

Standing water quickly degrades a finish and ultimately rots the wood. To prevent that, I drill two small drainage holes down in the groove between the lower curl and the panel. The holes exit the back of the sign so water has a place to escape. Handled properly, your house sign should provide many years of service.

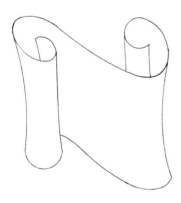
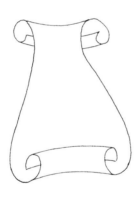

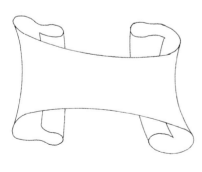

These drawings do not represent the scale of the original carvings in this article. They can be photocopied or redrawn to any desired size.

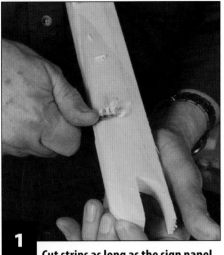

1 **Cut strips as long as the sign panel.** I used 2"-wide by ¾"-thick (50mm by 19mm) stock and rounded the curls with a carving knife and a block plane.

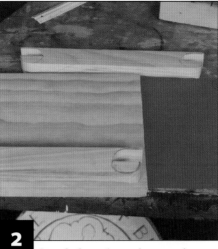

2 **Attach the strips** to the top and bottom of the panel with waterproof glue and screws inserted through the back of the panel.

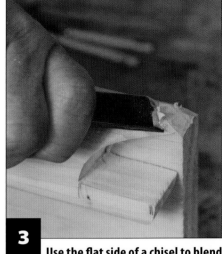

3 **Use the flat side of a chisel to blend the curls into the panel.**

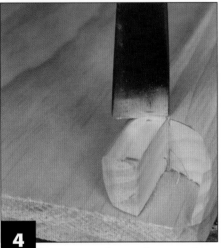

4 **Use a gouge that conforms to the curling edge of the roll and make a stop cut.** I used a #3 gouge here.

5 **With a fairly flat gouge, remove wood up to the stop cut made in the previous step.**

6 **You have many options when carving the ends of the curls,** including back cutting or undercutting slightly, as demonstrated here. This technique contributes to making a shadow, which suggests a hollow. To enhance the hollow, apply a dark stain before the finish coats.

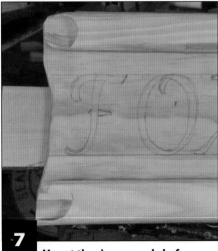

7 **Mount the sign securely before carving.** Here it is attached to a backing board held in a vise.

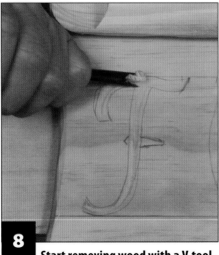

8 **Start removing wood with a V-tool.** Carve down the center of each letter or number, making sure the cutting edges of the V do not go outside the lines. Watch for grain changes and be prepared to reverse the cutting direction of the tool.

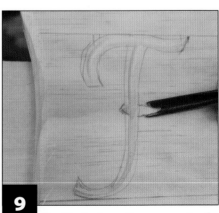

9 **Use the tool on all components of the letters,** including the long cross stroke on the F.

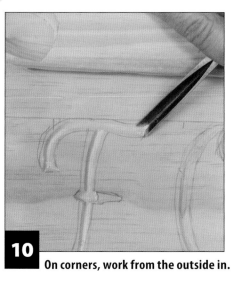

10 On corners, work from the outside in.

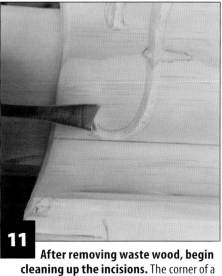

11 After removing waste wood, begin cleaning up the incisions. The corner of a #3 fishtail is useful on the end of a serif.

12 A knife with a narrow blade is an excellent choice for taking out a serif-corner chip.

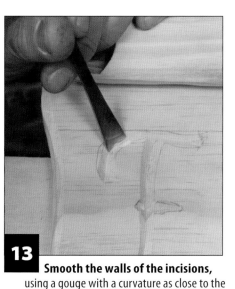

13 Smooth the walls of the incisions, using a gouge with a curvature as close to the letter outline as possible.

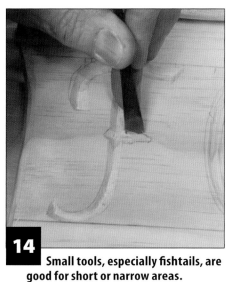

14 Small tools, especially fishtails, are good for short or narrow areas.

15 On convex lines, don't be tempted to turn the gouge over so that it is bevel up. Use a flat chisel or a #3 gouge with the bevel down; this keeps the corners from digging in.

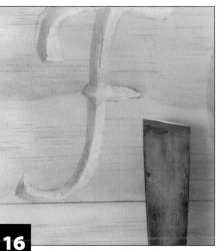

16 A slightly skewed chisel with gently rounded corners is excellent for cleaning up letters because it neatly slices the wood without corners catching in the grain.

17 Final cleanup with the skew chisel.

18 Where a chisel or gouge is impractical, use a knife for final cleanup.

Carving a House Sign

By Francis S. Lestingi

Producing a hand-carved, gold-leafed sign is a major achievement. These procedures and methods apply to signs of any size; following them, you could make anything from a large 40-square-foot church sign to a modest house sign.

The sign's design is the most important phase of the production. If the design is mediocre or generic, the finished product can be no better.

There are two approaches to carving a sign: carve first, then paint and gild later; or paint first, carve, then paint again and gild later. The former sounds like the simplest approach, but the latter is actually easier. We will use both techniques on different segments of this project.

I use only mahogany for signs and, despite the beauty of its rich grain, I coat it with paint, because a clear finish cannot withstand the elements as well as sign-industry primers and top coats. I use dark, rich, custom-mixed background colors to enhance the gold leaf.

1 **Cut the blank to shape.** Transfer the pattern to the blank. I use a laser print of the pattern and a heat pen transfer tool. You could also position carbon paper or graphite paper under a photocopy of the pattern and trace it onto the wood. Cut the design using a saber saw. Don't worry about the detailed areas yet; they will be refined with hand tools later.

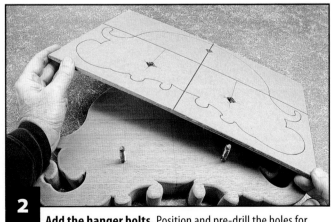

2 **Add the hanger bolts.** Position and pre-drill the holes for the hanger bolts. Twist the bolts in place with locking pliers. Use the bolts to make a cardboard template so you can easily position the holes for the bolts on the house. Hanger bolts are available at most hardware stores, sometimes in the plumbing section because they are often used to secure toilets to wooden floors.

3 **Make registration marks on the sides.** Remove the hanger bolts. Carve small nicks onto the sides to mark the centerlines before painting; it will save you the trouble of re-measuring later. This is particularly important with an oval shape because it is impossible to reestablish the major and minor axes of the oval after the carving is painted.

4 **Outline the cove.** The oval portion of the plaque has a cove that will be gilded later. Run a 3mm (⅛") 90° V-tool down the center of the cove. This provides a shallow root line or centerline for the entire cove. To enhance the reflectivity of the gold leaf, it is very important to keep the depth of incised letters, numbers, lines, and scrolls as shallow as possible.

5 **Carve the oval.** Use a 12mm (½") #1 chisel on the inner, or concave, side of the curve. Start at the black line and end at the root line. On the outer or convex side of the oval, use a 25mm (1") #2 gouge, again starting at the black line and ending at the root line.

6 **Carve the scrolls.** Repeat steps 4 and 5 to carve the scrolls. Use the same V-tool to establish the root line. The gouge sizes and sweeps, and the chisel sizes, will depend on the tightness of the curves in the scrolls, but the general carving procedure is the same regardless of the shape of the curves.

7 **Prime the sign.** Apply three coats of a sign-industry, water-based primer. Sand with 120-grit sandpaper between coats to ensure a smooth finish. Use two containers and tint one with a universal tint. Use the tinted primer for the second coat to ensure even coverage. Reinstall the hanger bolts to lift the panel off the bench so you can paint both sides and the back can dry.

8 **Apply the top coat.** Because a sign is typically exposed to the elements, it needs a high-quality top coat. I use a sign-industry, oil-based, high-gloss paint. Each coat requires 24 hours to dry. Rough up the surface of the paint with synthetic steel wool between coats. Again, different colors are used to distinguish between coats.

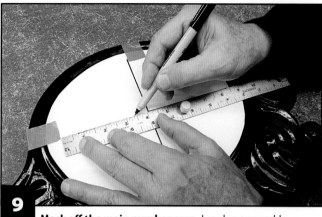

9 **Mask off the main number area.** I apply a removable vinyl mask with a plastic squeegee. The mask can be carved through and will simplify the gilding process. Use masking tape to transfer the registration marks to the mask and draw centerlines to help position the pattern.

10 **Attach a copy of the number pattern.** Photocopy or trace the numbers onto vellum tracing paper. Apply spray adhesive to the back of the vellum pattern and use the registration marks and centerlines to position the pattern. Use a plastic squeegee to press the pattern firmly in place.

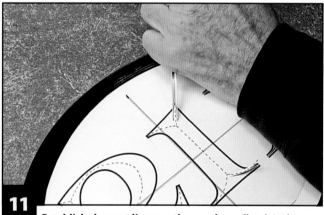

11 **Establish the root lines on the numbers.** Sketch in the lines representing the lowest part of the number and carve along the lines with a small V-tool, making shallow cuts. Eventually, with practice, you will be able to carve the root lines without penciling them in first.

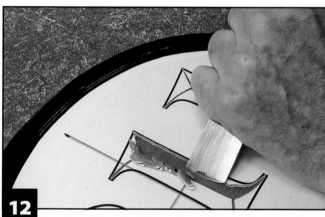

12 **Rough out the straight sections.** Make shallow cuts with a 25mm (1") #2 gouge, working from the edge in toward the root line. If a cut ends below the root line, the carving is too deep. Try to ride the bevel, keeping the cuts shallow by lowering the angle of the tool immediately after it initially bites into the wood.

13 **Rough out the serifs.** The triangular segment characteristic of Roman numbers and letters is called the *serif*. Numbers and letters that do not have serifs are referred to as *sans serif*. Serif letters look traditional and sans serif letters look modern. Use a 12mm (1") #2 gouge to rough out the serifs, using the technique explained in step 12.

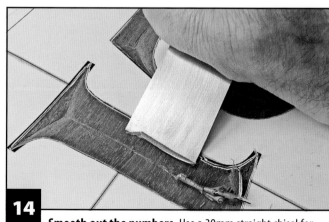

14 **Smooth out the numbers.** Use a 30mm straight chisel for the large areas and a 12mm (½") straight chisel for the serifs. Keep the cuts shallow by riding the bevel. It is often easier to produce a deep cut than a shallow one. You may slightly undercut an adjacent surface to produce a crisp line at the intersection of two surfaces at the centerline of the number.

15 **Carve the concave side of the curved numbers.** Carve the root line. Then use a 12mm (½") #2 gouge to carve down to the root line. Start ¼" (6mm) from the root line and follow the direction determined by the wood grain. Make additional passes, working ½" (13mm) from the root line, etc., until you reach the border line.

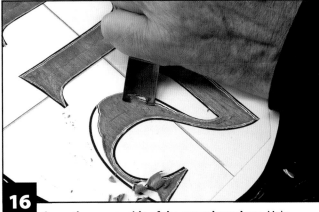

16 **Carve the convex side of the curved numbers.** Make short cuts around the curve, following the appropriate direction determined by the wood grain. Work in stages as you did in step 15. Smooth the surface using gouges for the curved areas and chisels for the flat areas. Carve the serifs with the same tool.

17 **Smooth the sides of the curved segments.** Start near the root line and proceed to the border, making the final smoothing cuts. Match the gouge's sweep to the curve, and change sweeps when necessary; most numbers and letters do not maintain a constant curvature. I started with a 20mm (¾") #5 gouge and then switched to a 25mm (1") #2 gouge where the curvature in 2 flattens near the serif.

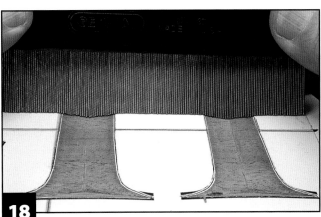

18 **Check the depth of your letters.** These are very shallow, with the depth of the root line slightly more than ⅛". With gilding, light reflects off shallow incised surfaces far more readily than it does deeply carved letters. Shallow numbers also require less gold.

MATERIALS:
- High-quality vellum tracing paper
- Carbon paper or graphite transfer paper (optional)
- ¾" x 12" x 18" (19mm x 300mm x 450mm) mahogany panel
- 3 each 3" (76mm)-long hanger bolts
- 14" x 20" (350mm x 500mm) piece of cardboard
- Sandpaper, 120 grit
- Synthetic steel wool
- Primer
- High-gloss oil-based paint
- Removable vinyl
- Spray adhesive

Materials & Tools

TOOLS:
- Heat transfer tool (optional)
- Saber saw with scroll blade
- Locking pliers
- 1" (25mm) red sable brush
- Plastic squeegee
- 3mm (⅛") 90° V-tool
- #1 chisels, 12mm and 30mm (½" and ¼")
- 25mm (1") #2 gouge
- 20mm (¾") #5 gouge

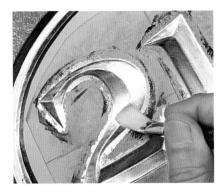

Gilding
The carved sign is now ready for the gold leafing or gilding process.

Pattern is drawn to scale on a 1" grid. Enlarge or reduce to desired size.

© 2011 Woodcarving Illustrated

A sign for all seasons

By Robert Merkel

I recently carved a house sign for a friend. He couldn't decide on a single design to accent the numbers, so I created a series of decorative panels that can be changed to fit the season.

Step 1: Create the interchangeable panels. Draw a 9" by 15" (230mm x 400mm) ellipse on a piece of plywood to act as the master pattern. Drill the screw holes and cut the oval blank. Use the master pattern and a router with a flush trim bit to produce a series of identical panels.

Step 2: Create the area for the panel. Trace the master pattern onto the main sign and use a router to remove ⅝" (16mm) of wood from the main sign to accommodate the panels.

Step 3: Add the mounting studs. Use the master pattern to determine the location of the mounting studs on the main sign. Drill pilot holes and insert the threaded bolts. You can put the completed panels on the sign quickly with a pair of wing nuts.

Step 4: Carve and paint the panels. Carve panels to represent specific holidays or the sign owner's personal interests. Finish each panel with a weather-resistant paint; I use oil-based enamel.

Gilding a House Sign

By Francis S. Lestingi

Gilding is the ancient art of applying a thin layer of metal to a surface. In carving, gilding is most often done using gold leaf, although silver and other metals can be used.

The creation of a carved and gilded sign, such as a residential plaque, can be approached in two ways. One method entails carving directly on the bare wood, coating the panel, and then applying the size (adhesive) and gold leaf. The problem with this approach is that the application of the size requires considerable skill and time. An easier method uses removable vinyl masks. With this method, the wood panel is completely painted first. The vinyl is applied to the painted surface and the carving is done directly through the vinyl and painted wood. The carved areas are then painted and sized. With the vinyl serving as a mask, the process is effortless.

Size is available in two curing speeds—fast (1-hour curing time) and slow (12-hour curing time). Slow-curing size produces a more brilliant gild, especially if it is allowed to cure for 48 hours. Gold leaf is available in loose-leaf form and in patent form. Patent gold is attached to tissue sheets, comes in booklets of 25 sheets, and is novice-friendly. After you become comfortable with the gilding process, I recommend learning to use loose-leaf gold.

The numbers on the sign are carved through a vinyl mask, allowing us to use the easier method of gold leafing. The scrolls do not use a vinyl mask and will be gilded using the alternate method. Patent gold leaf is used in both instances to simplify the process.

Installing the sign

Use the template created in the carving article to position the sign. Place the template on the wall and mark the holes. Drill into the wall with a bit that is twice the diameter of the hanger bolt. Clean out the holes and fill them with silicone caulk. Add some silicone on the back of the panel and insert the bolts into the holes. Do not apply a finish over the gold leaf. Genuine 23-karat (or higher) gold leaf used in an exterior application is impervious to the elements. Coating the gold leaf will immediately lessen the luster drastically and will cause the gold leaf to crack as the coating or finish decays. Nothing is as good as gold.

Materials & Tools

MATERIALS:
- Primer
- High-gloss oil-based paint
- Sandpaper, 120 grit
- Kaolin, USP
- Slow size
- 23k patent gold leaf
- Rubbing alcohol

TOOLS:
- 1" (25mm)-wide red sable brush (apply paint)
- Dusting mop
- #0 and #5 lettering quill brushes
- Gilder's mop
- White sable brush of choice
- Scissors
- Hobby knife

1 Prime and paint the numbers. Apply three coats of primer. Sand lightly between coats with 120-grit sandpaper. Apply two coats of sign-industry oil-based high-gloss paint. Let the paint dry for 24 hours between coats. High-gloss paint produces a brilliant gild. Use satin paint for a matte gild. Sand the surface around the numbers lightly with 120-grit sandpaper to remove any paint buildup.

2 Dust the surface with kaolin USP. Vacuum up the sanding dust, wipe it with a paper towel, and vacuum again. Spatter the kaolin, a pure powder form of the mineral kaolite, on the entire surface of the sign and smooth it out with an artist mop brush. Vacuum away any excess dust. The kaolin make the colorless size visible and prevents gold leaf from adhering to the painted areas on the cove and scroll that are not intended to be gilded.

3 **Apply size to the numbers.** Pick up a small amount of size on a ½" (13mm)-wide white sable artist's brush. Stroke the brush on a glossy magazine page to distribute the size thinly and evenly throughout the brush. Apply the size to the numbers. The size absorbs the kaolin and produces a visible glossy coating. Make sure the coating of size is thin, complete, and uniform. Remove any puddles in the valleys.

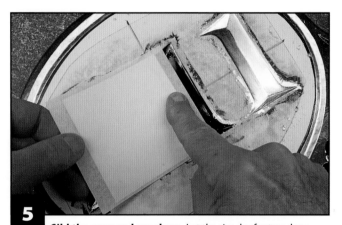

5 **Gild the cove and numbers.** Let the size dry for two days. Start at the top of the cove and work your way around. Place a sheet of gold leaf facedown on the size and press lightly. The gold should rest on top of the size, but not be submerged in it. The gold peels off the paper as it sticks to the size. Gild the numbers, pressing lightly on one side of the number and then the other.

6 **Burnish the gold leaf.** Use a white sable brush. *Burnish* refers to cleaning up the edges and removing any overlapping gold leaf. Never touch the gold with your fingers; the more you touch it, the less brilliant it will be. Use the brush to lightly press the gold leaf against the size where necessary. Eventually, the size will harden with the gold leaf atop it.

4 **Apply size to the cove and scrolls.** Use a professional lettering quill brush. This brush remains a constant width as you draw it around the curves. Use a #5 brush for the coves and a #0 brush for the scrolls. Take your time and be careful as you apply the size. Because these areas are not carved through a vinyl mask, the surrounding surface is not protected. The gold leaf will adhere to any area where size is applied.

7 **Apply gold leaf to the scrolls.** Use the method explained in step 5. The kaolin prevents the gold from sticking to the relatively fresh paint. Use a soft gilder's mop to burnish the scrolls. The mop also removes the excess kaolin dust. If the kaolin sticks to the paint, remove it with a paper towel moistened with rubbing alcohol. Do not touch the gold with the alcohol.

TOUCHING UP   **TIP**

Small voids where the gold leaf does not adhere properly are called holidays. If the gold leaf does not adhere when you attempt to cover holidays, you may have to re-size and re-gild these areas. Fast size works if the holiday is small enough.

8   **Remove the vinyl mask.** Use a hobby knife to lift up a corner of the mask. Pull the vinyl at a 90° angle to the gold-leafed edge. Cut the mask with scissors at strategic places, such as the serifs, to facilitate crisp clean edges. If you pull the mask toward the gilded section, it may lift some of the gold. Always remove the vinyl mask perpendicular to the gilded edge, not toward it.

GILDING WITH LOOSE LEAF   **TIP**

While the surface preparation is the same, the process of gilding with loose-leaf gold requires a different approach than gilding with patent gold. Loose-leaf gold is heavier than patent gold. It also provides a more brilliant gild. In a high-relief carving, loose-leaf gold will provide better coverage than patent gold.

Gilding with Loose Leaf

1   **Charge the brush.** Dab a bit of lip balm on your hand and brush a gilder's tip (a specialized brush) over the oiled hand. The brush picks up a bit of oil, which attracts the gold leaf.

2   **Cut the gold leaf.** Full sheets of gold leaf are rarely used. Cut the full sheet into smaller segments with a gilder's knife.

3   **Apply the gold leaf.** Transfer the gold leaf to the sized surface using the gilder's tip lightly charged with lip balm. The gold leaf is more attracted to the size than to the oil on the brush, so it will easily transfer to the size.

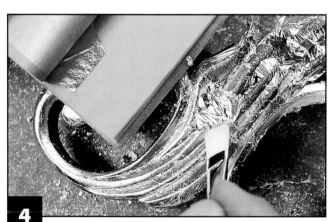

4   **Burnish the gold leaf.** Tear off small pieces of gold leaf with a white sable brush and fill any small voids or holes. Burnish the gold leaf with the same brush using the techniques explained in step 6 on page 110.

Custom Presentation Plaque

By Floyd L. Truitt

A hand-carved plaque makes a much stronger impression than generic commercially available trophies.

This versatile design allows you to customize the plaque with relief-carved elements pertinent to the recipient or award. The designs used on this plaque are applicable for a number of awards, but feel free to personalize the plaque with your own designs. You can use the symbol for a profession, a specific hobby or interest, or even your carving club's logo.

Once you learn the techniques for the scroll work, you'll be able to carve the basic plaque fairly quickly, and can concentrate on the relief-carved elements. I designed this piece to serve as an award plaque for a carving show and sized the plate area to fit a 3" x 5" (75mm x 130mm) plate, but you can size the insert area to match any plate. I begin by using a router equipped with a keyhole bit to cut a hanging slot centered on the back of the plaque, 4" (100mm) down from the top. If you prefer, you can add a conventional hanger to the back after completing the project.

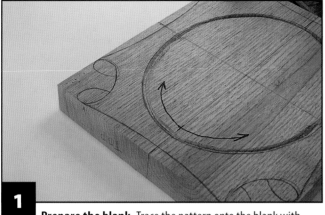

1 **Prepare the blank.** Trace the pattern onto the blank with graphite paper. Carve along the oval with an 8mm (⁵⁄₁₆") V-tool. Stay inside the marked line. Because of the grain, you have to carve in two directions, shown by the arrows on the blank.

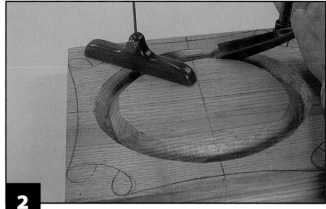

2 **Enlarge the groove.** Switch to a 60° 26mm (1") V-tool and use a mallet to carve the groove ⅝" (16mm)-deep. The groove should be a uniform depth the whole way around the oval. I use a shop-made depth gauge, but you can use a combination square or a ruler.

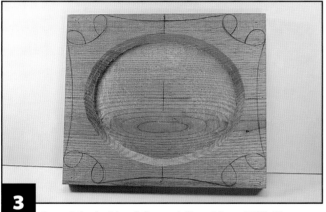

3 **Round the inside of the oval.** Use a 30mm (1¼") #5 gouge. Start at the groove and work toward the center. The oval will end up looking somewhat like a football. Establish the shape, round the oval, then remove the tool marks with 120-grit sandpaper.

4 **Round the outside of the groove.** Round the sides of the groove with a 35mm (1⅜") #3 gouge. Remove the tool marks from the #3 gouge with a 35mm (1⅜") #2 gouge. You want a smooth, even transition from the border to the oval.

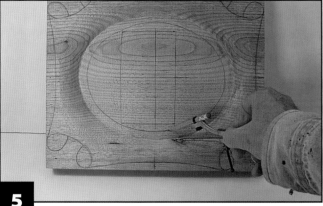

5 **Mark the inner oval.** Set a compass to ½" (13mm). Follow the bottom of the groove with the leg of the compass, and draw another oval inside the first one. Mark the area for the engraved 3" x 5" (75mm x 130mm) plate.

6 **Cut the perimeter to shape.** Use a band saw to cut along the outside pattern lines to establish the general shape. It is possible to remove this wood by hand, but a band saw speeds the process.

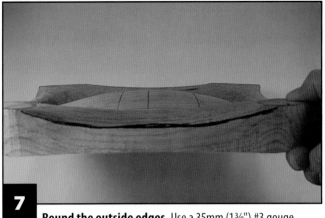

7 **Round the outside edges.** Use a 35mm (1⅜") #3 gouge. Blend the outside edges into the cuts you made in step 4. Remove the tool marks with a 35mm (1⅜") #2 gouge. The four corners where the scroll will be carved remain the high points.

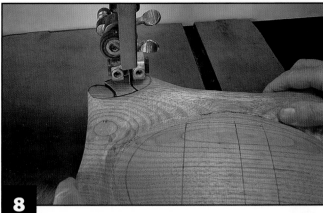

8 **Cut the outline of the scrolls.** Use a band saw. Be careful: the orientation of the grain makes some of these areas fragile. You want to remove the negative space between the two curls on each corner.

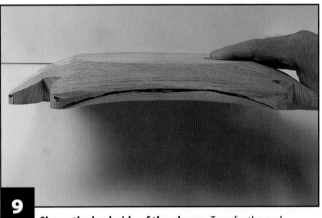

9 **Shape the back side of the plaque.** Transfer the oval from the pattern to the back of the plaque. Round the edges on the outside of the oval so the back is convex. Use a 35mm (1⅜") #3 gouge, then remove the tool marks from the #3 gouge with a 35mm (1⅜") #2 gouge. Keep the area inside the oval flat so it lays correctly against the wall.

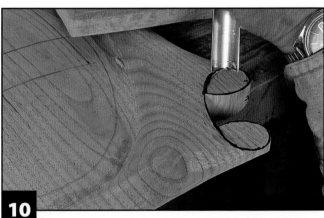

10 **Shape the first curl.** Use an 18mm (¾") #8 gouge. Start at the highest point, with the gouge nearly perpendicular to the wood. Push and twist the gouge along the line to carefully scoop out the wood. Make small cuts to prevent the wood from chipping out. Use a 16mm (⅝") #9 gouge in the tighter spots. Practice the technique on scrap wood first.

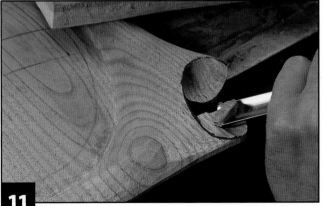

11 **Finish shaping the curls on the scroll.** Use a 18mm (¾") #8 gouge and a similar technique to shape the opposite curl on the corner of the scroll. Repeat steps 10 and 11 to shape both curls on the remaining three corners of the scroll.

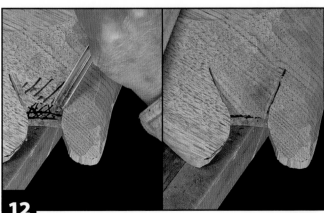

12 **Remove wood from the back near the scrolls.** Make stop cuts around the shaded area with an 8mm (⁵⁄₁₆") V-tool. Remove the wood between the stop cuts with a 12mm (½") #5 gouge. These cuts make the scrolls more realistic.

13 **Carve a groove around the inner oval line.** Use an 8mm (¾") V-tool. Carve the groove ¹⁄₁₆" (2mm) deep. Make a stop cut around the 3" x 5" (76mm x 127mm) plate area with a 35mm (1⅜") straight chisel. Remove the wood between the stop cuts with a 35mm (1⅜") #3 gouge.

14 **Add the low relief embellishments.** I provided a generic pattern for a carving plaque, but I usually personalize the plaque using a family coat of arms, a corporate logo, or even a military insignia. Use your tools of choice.

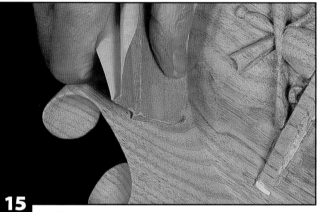

15 **Sand the entire carving.** Use 150-grit sandpaper, then switch to 240- or 320-grit. Remove the sanding dust with compressed air or a tack cloth.

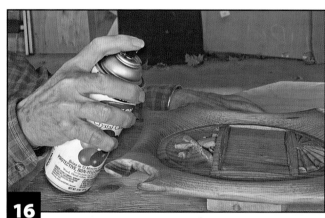

16 **Apply the finish.** I use clear satin acrylic spray finish. Apply five or six coats from all directions. Sand lightly between coats with 600-grit sandpaper.

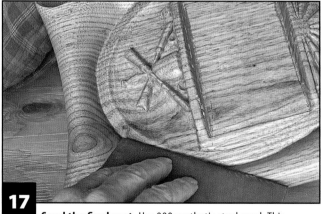

17 **Sand the final coat.** Use 000 synthetic steel wool. This removes any dust that adhered to the finish and produces a very smooth surface. 3" x 5" (75mm x 130mm) plaques can be purchased and engraved at most trophy shops. Attach the plaque with screws or epoxy.

MATERIALS:
- 1⅜" x 10" x 12" (35mm x 254mm x 305mm) butternut or wood of choice
- Sandpaper, assorted grits between 120 and 600
- 000 synthetic steel wool
- Finish of choice
- 3" x 5" (75mm x 130mm) engraved plate

TOOLS:
- Straight and skew chisels: 6 or 8mm, 12mm, and 35mm (¼" or ⁵⁄₁₆", ½" and 1⅜")

Materials & Tools

- 35mm (1⅜") #2 and #3 gouges
- 30mm (1³⁄₁₆") #5 gouge
- 18mm (¾") #8 gouge
- 16mm (⅝") #9 gouge
- 8mm (⁵⁄₁₆") V-tool
- 60° 26mm (1") V-tool
- 20mm (¾") #3 gouge
- 12mm (½") #5 gouge
- Assorted fishtail and micro chisels and gouges (relief carving)
- Compass and depth gauge
- Band saw

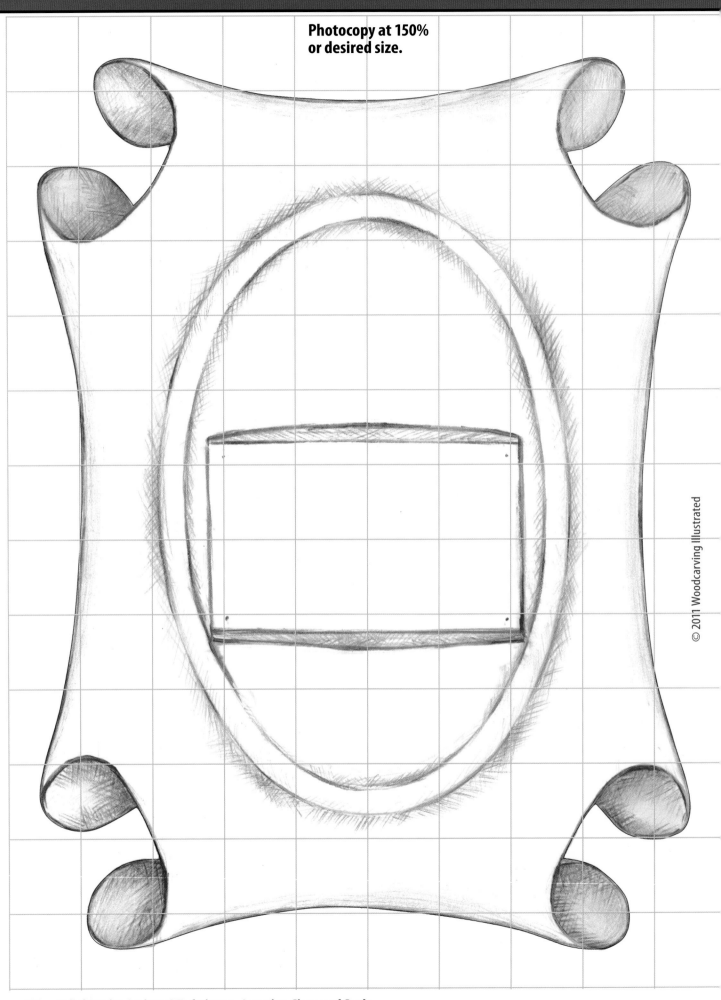

Photocopy at 150% or desired size.

© 2011 Woodcarving Illustrated

Photocopy at 100% or desired size.

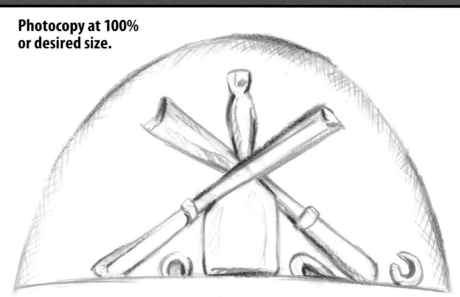

Making it personal

With a bit of creativity and imagination, you can customize the relief parts of the plaque for nearly any situation. Use the symbol for a profession, such as doctor or lawyer, to acknowledge accomplishments such as passing the bar exam. Carve a bowling ball and pins to commemorate a 300 score, or a baseball bat and glove to celebrate a first home run.

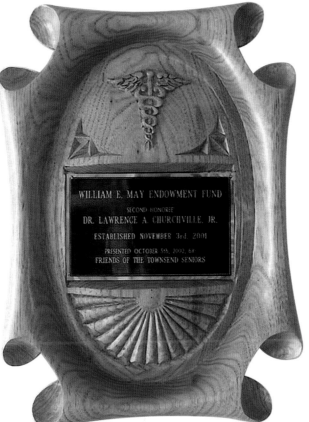

Print Your Own Holiday Cards

By Bob Duncan

For a fun twist on relief carving, make your own holiday cards using traditional block printing techniques and this angel pattern Elaine Vardjan adapted from an 1807 weather vane of Gabriel and his announcing horn.

Elaine, a third-generation printer, carves image blocks for cards, bookplates, jar labels, and even linen towels and placemats, and Matt Vardjan prints them on the antique presses Elaine's great-uncle used.

Most carvers use pine or basswood for printing blocks. Elaine has done some work with wood blocks, but prefers battleship linoleum because it is much easier to carve and more durable. Unlike wood, it has no grain to contend with, and the texture is consistent throughout.

"If you put (the linoleum) out in the sun it gets to the consistency of hard butter," Elaine said. Wood block prints will make 150-200 prints before wearing out, "but linoleum will take thousands of smacks (from the printing press)."

One of the trickiest things about block printing is thinking in reverse.

"You have to know what to remove and what to keep. You want to keep the image," Elaine said.

You can use a press to make the image, but it will eventually damage the block, so many people press their images by hand.

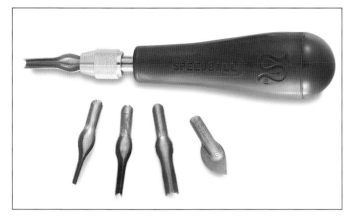

Linoleum Gouges Vs. Wood Gouges

You can use traditional woodcarving gouges on linoleum, but because it is so much softer than wood, special linoleum gouges allow you to turn tighter corners and create sharper images without resorting to using a knife. Linoleum gouges like the ones shown here are much thinner and finer than traditional wood gouges.

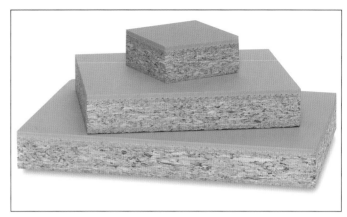

Battleship Linoleum vs. Regular Linoleum

Battleship linoleum is not the same vinyl flooring you find in your kitchen. Made of corkboard and linseed oil, the linoleum is backed with burlap. Attached to a wood backing here, it is also available separately.

UNDERCUTTING THE EDGE

The V-tool works best to outline the angel, following the curves easily and keeping you from "undercutting" the edge. If you undercut the edge, it will collapse and the block will be ruined. Think of a stream bank—if the stream cuts away under the bank, it will collapse if you walk on it. The same principle applies to block printing.

EASY INK PLATE **TIP**

Any piece of glass or acrylic will work for the ink plate. Just add a little ink to the plate and roll the brayer across it until it is fully inked.

1 Trace the angel pattern onto the basswood or linoleum.

2 Using a V-tool or carving knife, outline both sides of the angel's legs and feet.

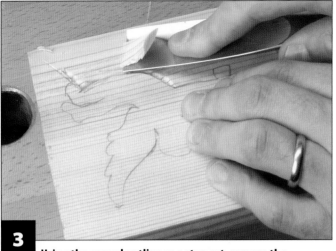

3 **Using the carved outline as a stop cut, remove the waste from around the angel** using a gouge. Don't worry about the marks left behind by the gouge; they won't be visible when the block image is printed. The angel image should be raised at least ⅛" (3mm) above the surrounding wood for a good print.

4 **Outline the angel's arms, scroll, and trumpet.** The carving knife works best to cut in the straight lines both with and across the grain.

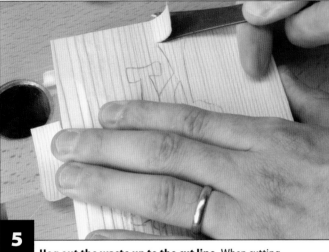

5 **Hog out the waste up to the cut line.** When cutting across the grain, be careful not to cut too far and gouge the work piece. Weak sections, such as the flared ends of the trumpet and the angel's feet, can be strengthened by soaking the area with super glue.

6 **Carve in the outline of the area between the angel's arm and the trumpet.** Again, the knife works best to cut these straight lines. A few quick cuts with the knife clears out the waste. It doesn't matter what the block's bottom looks like; as long as the raised image is right, the print will work.

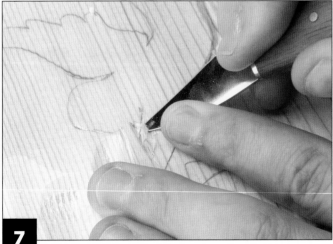

7 **Carve out the outline of the angel's face** with the knife before hogging off the waste with the gouge.

8 **Outline the front of the wings and clear away the waste.** Move on to the tip of the wing and the feather details.

9 **Carefully shape the angel's wings,** making sure to keep the rounded image. Clear away the waste to leave the raised image.

10 **Roll the brayer on an inked plate** until it is covered with ink.

11 **Roll the inked brayer over the angel image,** making sure the whole thing is inked.

12 **Press the absorbent paper down on the inked image.** Rub across the back of the paper with a wooden spoon or similar tool. Carefully lift the inked paper straight up off the block. If you shift the paper at all the ink will smear and ruin the image. Alternately, you can flip the block over and press it onto the paper.

Photocopy at 100%

MATERIALS:
- 3" x 5" (75mm x 130mm) block of basswood or 3" x 5" (75mm x 130mm) piece of battleship linoleum
- Ink color of choice
- Absorbent paper

Materials & Tools

TOOLS:
- ⅛" (3mm) 60° V-tool
- Gouge
- Carving knife or set of linoleum gouges
- Ink pad or brayer and ink plate

Patterns

This is the place to let your imagination run free. Use these patterns to add relief carving to existing wooden items or as inspiration to create entirely new projects. Use them whole or select part of a design for a simple carving or to customize a different pattern. No reproduction percentages are given—adjust the size as needed. Most carvers use the outline pattern for layout and the shaded pattern to determine depth. The shaded versions can also serve as woodburning patterns—and, as several of the designers point out, you can easily adapt them for other forms of carving, too.

Lighthouse
by Lora S. Irish
page 13

Celtic Knotwork

By Wayne Cruze

When carving knotwork designs, remember that if one "ribbon" goes under another, it needs to look continuous, with the same width, depth, and curve. Precision and exactness are important.

My daughter's Irish dancing inspired me to start carving Celtic knotwork. I carve all my pieces by hand, usually in basswood, which is easy to work with and holds detail well.

Celtic Hearts

By Wayne Cruze

I carved this as a basswood basket lid and finished it with a stain/wax combination finish, which gives more depth and dimension than any other finishes I've tried.

Quilt Squares

By Cyndi Joslyn

I never seem to find time to quilt with fabric, but I can always find time to carve. These squares are based on traditional quilt block designs.

This is a great project to practice your knife control—wearing a carving glove and thumb guard, of course.

I use acrylic paints on these, but you can use acrylic fluids for a more transparent effect. I finish them with a water-based laquer and antiquing gel.

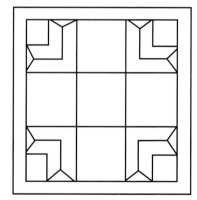

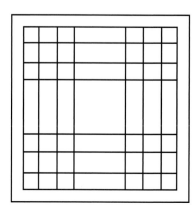

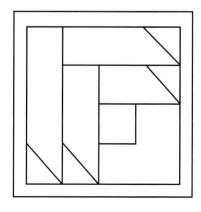

Covered Bridge Scene

By Dean Troutman

I hand-carve all my pieces and finish many of them with oil paints and wood stains, which give a soft, subtle finish that is easy to control and apply.

Rustic Barn Scene

By Lora S. Irish

Landscapes, so forgiving of pattern line changes, are excellent for new carvers learning how to make cuts, which tools work best, and how wood grain affects the direction and depth of a cut. Here, sides and roofs of the buildings are the few straight lines that require special attention.

Small projects like this are perfect for carving in your lap with hand tools, using a heavy terry cloth towel to protect your lap and catch wood chips. I used a basic beginner's carving set with a large and a small round gouge, a small V-tool, a straight and a skew chisel, and a basic bench knife.

Acorn Relief

By Lora S. Irish

This design can be used as a stand-alone carving or to embellish a sign.

The combination of rich texture and smooth surfaces lends instant appeal, with the deep undercuts tucking the joints back out of sight and making the acorn stand out from the background, giving additional dimension.

Harvest Maiden

By Lora S. Irish

This charming nostalgic design is the perfect embellishment for a bread box. The image makes a stunning presentation when carved in a light wood, such as basswood or butternut, and can be highlighted with subtle colors or finished naturally.

Beginners may find the delicate ribbons and flowing lines difficult to render as a traditional relief carving. Adapt the design to your interests and skill level—it can also work as a simple line carving, intaglio carving (where the subject is recessed into the background), free-form chip carving, or woodburning.

Santa and Snowman

By Lora S. Irish

These look equally good painted or with a natural finish. Not too complicated, they are great projects to mass-produce for holiday presents. Paint them different colors to have a whole host.

Make the hat hooks a little larger and slip them over doorknobs, or add hangers to the back and hang them on walls or doors. Reduce the size for cheerful tree ornaments or add pin backs for festive brooches.

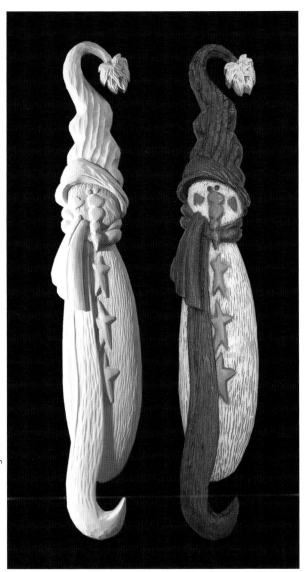

Santa Claus

By Lora S. Irish

French Horn

By Lora S. Irish

Christmas Presents

By Lora S. Irish

This heartwarming pairing of lamb and puppy is suited for relief carving, bas relief, or woodburning.

Use the whole design to embellish a plaque or napkin holder, or separate the individual elements to use the lamb for a baby's room and the puppy for animal lovers. The Christmas balls could be borders on other projects or, centered on a small square, a delightful ornament.

Add subtle color to the completed carving or woodburning with watercolors or thinned acrylic paints.

Eagle Plaque

By Lora S. Irish

Use this versatile design for low- or high-relief carving or for woodburning. Personalize the open area below the eagle with a name and rank to honor a member of the armed forces or a surname and house number.

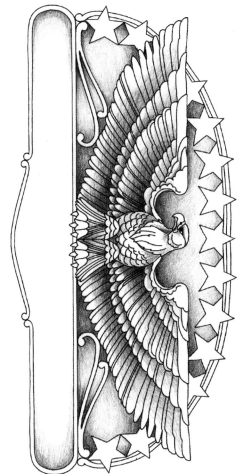

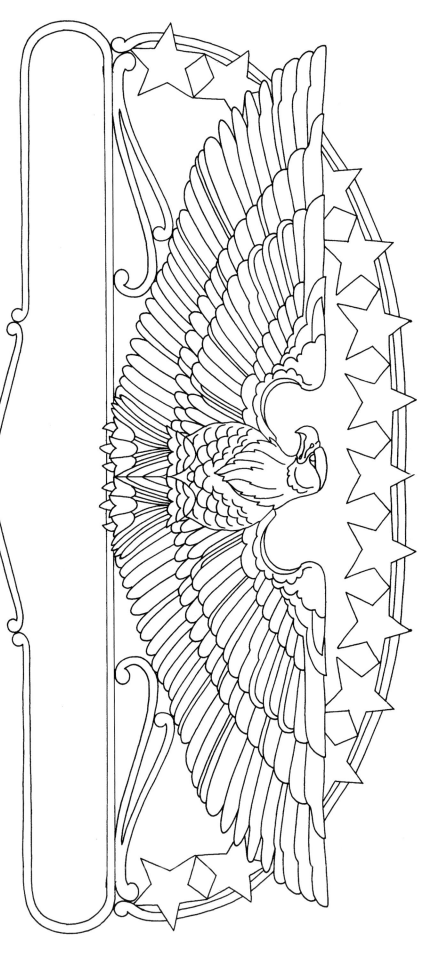

Pintail Duck in Cattails

By Lora S. Irish

Whether you're a hunter or a nature lover, this classic waterfowl scene is a perfect way to immortalize those serene days by the lake.

With a few slight modifications, it's easy to turn the design into a welcome sign or an artistic way to display your house number. It would also be a great way to display a few feathers from your latest trophy.

Lighthouse

By Lora S. Irish

Maple Leaf Greenman

By Lora S. Irish

This profile pattern can be used to decorate any number of items. It is the perfect design for a set of bookends or the brackets that hold a mantel in place. It is also an ideal embellishment for a garden chair or other furniture.

The pattern denoting suggested levels of relief carving is to assist you in roughing out your project. Level 1 is the highest point of the carving (where the least amount of wood is removed), and level 4 is the lowest level of the carving (where the most wood is removed).

Home Sweet Home

By Lora S. Irish

This pattern is suitable for traditional relief carving, but don't be afraid to try something new with it. Try adding color to the birds, carving the birds separately and attaching them to the board, or recessing the letters and carving the birds in relief.

Contributors

Robert Biermann
Robert, of Missouri, puts his decades of carving experience to use teaching. He has won awards at shows including the International Woodcarvers Congress.
twodulbug@sbcglobal.net
www.johnsworldofcarving.com

Wayne Cruze
Wayne, of Ohio, began carving as a hobby and now estimates he has sold or given away thousands of pieces.
www.celticcarving.com

Bob Duncan
Bob, of Pennsylvania, is technical editor of *Woodcarving Illustrated* and *Scroll Saw Woodworking & Crafts*.

Jim Dupont
Jim, of Indiana, a retired woodworking and drafting teacher, especially enjoys relief carvings and caricature figures, for which he consistently wins awards.

Andy Fairchok
Andy, of Arizona, a retired IBM systems designer, now spends his time as a carving instructor, writer, and distributor for woodcarving books and tools.

Dave Hamilton
Dave, of Colorado, an ecologist by profession, particularly enjoys carving birds. With Chuck Solomon, he has written several books for Fox Chapel Publishing.
www.foxchapelpublishing.com

Lora S. Irish
Lora, of Maryland, writes *Woodcarving Illustrated's* Relief Column and has written numerous woodworking and craft books for Fox Chapel Publishing.
www.carvingpatterns.com

Mary-Ann Jack-Bleach
Mary-Ann, of Ontario, Canada, taught herself to relief carve in 1979. She now teaches and judges woodcarving and has pieces in collections throughout the world.
mableach@execulink.com

Cyndi Joslyn
Cyndi, of Idaho, is a Santa collector and carver. She teaches carving and has written several books for Fox Chapel Publishing.
cyndijoslyn@gmail.com

W.F. Judt
Bill, an ordained pastor and full-time carver, is from Saskatchewan, Canada. Specializing in relief carving, he teaches others and has written several books for Fox Chapel Publishing.
www.wwwoodcarver.com

Francis S. Lestingi
Francis, of New York, traces his interest in lettering and gilding back to elementary school. In 1994 he retired from a physics professorship to start a sign-carving business with his son.
www.signsofgold.com

Robert Merkel
Robert, of Massachusetts, is a mechanical designer who has been carving for about 40 years.

Jerry Mifflin
Jerry, of Arizona, a lifelong artist in oils, watercolors, and pencil, left the telecommunications industry in 2001 and now creates custom deep-relief mantels and other large pieces.
www.jerrymifflinwoodcarving.com

Charley Phillips
Charley, of Texas, started as a decorative painter and turned to carving in 1995. She is known for her delicate floral carvings and female caricature carvings.
www.charleyphillips.com

Judy Ritger
Judy, of Wisconsin, teaches painting and carving around the country.
www.pinewoodforge.com

Chuck Solomon
Chuck, of Colorado, a terrestrial ecologist by profession, particularly enjoys making carvings of birds and animals. He teaches and judges woodcarving and has won more than 100 ribbons in shows. With Dave Hamilton, he has written several books for Fox Chapel Publishing.
www.foxchapelpublishing.com

Robert Stadtlander
Robert, of New York, is mostly self-taught and has been carving since 1990. Specializing in scenic relief carving, he has won numerous awards and teaches workshops.
www.stadtlandercarvings.com

Dean Troutman
Dean, of Missouri, has demonstrated carving in Silver Dollar City, an 1890s-style theme park, for more than 30 years.
deantroutman@gmail.com

Floyd Truitt
Floyd, of Massachusetts, started carving when he was 12 years old and has been carving full-time since retiring from the Federal Civil Service in 1986.
floydcarves@msn.com

Linda Tudor
Linda, of Illinois, was a health information administrator who particularly enjoyed using chip-carving and relief techniques on egg and globe shapes.
home.earthlink.net/~tudorart/

Christina White
Christina, of Georgia, operates a gallery and studio complex. Carving wood has been her sole artistic medium in recent years.
www.funkychickenartproject.com

Frederick Wilbur
Frederick, of Virginia, has written several books on decorative and architectural woodcarving that are available through Fox Chapel Publishing.
www.frederickwilbur-woodcarver.com

Kathy Wise
Kathy, of Michigan, started as a professional animal sculptor but is also known for her intarsia designs. She is a frequent magazine contributor and has written several books for Fox Chapel Publisher. Kathy Wise Designs Inc., P.O. Box 60, Yale, MI 48097; fax 810-387-9044.
kathywise@bignet.net
www.kathywise.com

Index

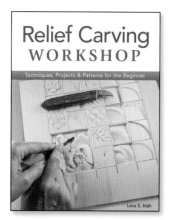

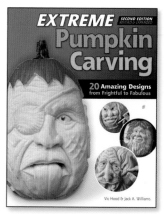
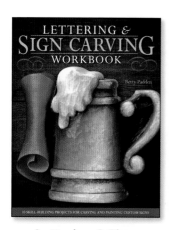

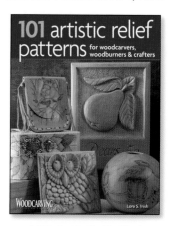